THE PARENTS' HANDBOOK ON SCHOOL TESTING

THE PARENTS' HANDBOOK ON SCHOOL TESTING

Ann E. Boehm and **Mary Alice White**

DEPARTMENT OF PSYCHOLOGY
TEACHERS COLLEGE, COLUMBIA UNIVERSITY

TEACHERS COLLEGE, COLUMBIA UNIVERSITY
NEW YORK AND LONDON   1982

Published by Teachers College Press, 1234 Amsterdam Avenue,
New York, N.Y. 10027

Library of Congress Cataloging in Publication Data

Boehm, Ann E., 1938–
  The parents' handbook on school testing.

  Bibliography: p.
  Includes index.
  1. Educational tests and measurements—
Handbooks, manuals, etc.   I. White, Mary Alice.
II. Title.
LB3051.B58   371.2'6   81-16700
ISBN 0-8077-2660-5   AACR2

Acknowledgments

Tables 1, 2, and 3 appeared originally in *The Chronicle of Higher Education*,
January 19, 1981. Reprinted with permission.
Copyright 1981 by *The Chronicle of Higher Education*.

CIRCUS 9: *Listen to the Story*, Sentence Report Table. Copyright 1978,
The Educational Testing Service. Reprinted by permission.

Stanford Achievement Test, Cover Page and Pupil Information Box.
Reproduced by permission. Copyright © 1972 by Harcourt Brace Jovanovich, Inc.
All rights reserved.

Manufactured in the United States of America

87   86   85   84   83   82   2   3   4   5   6

Contents

Introduction   v

1 The Ten Minute Parent-Teacher Conference   1

2 How to Read Achievement Test Scores and Reports   10

3 What Is an Intelligence Test? What Does an IQ Score Mean?   32

4 The Most Frequently Used Achievement Tests and What
   They Measure   45

5 Questions Parents Should Ask at School and How to Ask
   Them   54

6 Aptitude, Interest, and Personality Tests: What They Can
   and Cannot Do   68

7 What a Parent Needs to Know About School Records   73

8 John and Sheila and Henry and Vicki: Four Individual
   Children   90

9 What Are Preschool and Readiness Tests?   103

10 Testing the Child with Special Needs 116

11 Helping Your Child to Prepare for Tests and to Understand Test Results 126

12 Selecting a School for Your Child 140

13 The Questions Most Frequently Asked About Testing 159

Appendices 167

A. A Calendar of School Testing 168

B. Interpreting Grade Equivalent Scores 170

C. Percentiles and Their Numerical Meaning 172

D. Percentiles and Their Qualitative Meaning 173

E. Converting Stanines to Percentiles 174

F. If You Want More Information: Suggested Readings 175

G. Admissions Standards to Colleges 177

Glossary of Testing Terms 179

Index 187

Introduction

During their school years, children take many tests; readiness tests, achievement tests, IQ tests, weekly classroom tests, placement tests, and college admission tests. Most of these tests are administered to children in a group. Many decisions that schools make about your child are based on the results from such tests.

Our purpose in this book is to provide parents with accurate information about school testing. What do test scores mean? What questions should parents ask about test scores? What do different tests measure? What should parents know *before* they go to a school conference?

We have been on both sides of the school desk ourselves; as psychologists we have administered tests to children, counselled parents, and consulted with teachers and administrators. We have talked across the desk with parents, and we have talked from the other side of the desk as parents ourselves.

What we think parents need—and badly—is a guide to school tests, so we wrote this for them. We hope parents find it useful.

We wish to express our warm appreciation to Dan Oehlsen for his careful editorial assistance.

ANN E. BOEHM, PH.D
Professor of Psychology and Education

MARY ALICE WHITE, PH.D.
Professor of Psychology and Education

February 1982

CHAPTER 1

The Ten Minute Parent-Teacher Conference

In most elementary schools, parent-teacher conferences are held two or three times a year. At a regularly scheduled time, the parent or parents, usually the mother, meets the teacher for approximately ten minutes to review her child's progress. These regular parent-teacher conferences were invented to provide parents with a chance to talk with their child's teacher and to discuss any common problems that parent and teacher might have. The idea behind them is a very good one because it does provide some regularly scheduled face-to-face time for teachers and parents to talk. Like most good ideas, it has certain problems in execution. One problem is that with only a few minutes allotted to each parent, the interviews tend to be rather superficial. It is hard for a teacher, who has some 25 or 30 conferences scheduled in one week, to be profound about a child in ten minutes. (We use the feminine gender for elementary teachers because it is the most probable and because citing two genders throughout is awkward.) Parents are usually happy to hear from the teacher that things are going well, or that the teacher is not having any particular problem with their child.

The Teacher's Viewpoint

We might look at these conferences, first, from the point of view of the school and the teacher. Imagine, if you can, being the teacher of 25 or 35 third grade children and facing the parent conference week that is coming up! You are probably nervous and tense about meeting 25 or 35 mothers and/or fathers who are going to be concerned about their child,

1

about whom you are supposed to be quite knowledgeable. It is very hard for you to keep all the information about each child in your head. You want to make a good impression on the parents because you want them to feel that their child is being taught by a competent person. You also want to develop a good working relationship with the parents in case you need their help at home on a specific problem. As a teacher, particularly if you are a young teacher, it is one of the most trying parts of the year for you. What teachers dread more than anything else is criticism from parents. Their idea of a nightmare is to have belligerent parents come in and accuse them of not doing a good job with their child. This, of course, puts teachers on the defensive and makes them feel as if their efforts were totally unappreciated. Criticism or hostility from parents is very hard for teachers to handle, and understandably so. Principals also do not like difficult, hostile, or litigious parents, or those who criticize the school. Parents who act this way are seen as the enemy by almost everyone on the school staff.

How to Prepare for the Conference

In approaching your parent-teacher conference, as a parent, the first thing to remember is to handle it in such a way that you remain on good terms with the teacher, no matter what your opinion might be of her. She may be the best teacher in the world, or she may not be. She may be doing the best teaching job in the world, or she may not. But she is going to be your child's teacher for the rest of the year, and she may be doing the very best she knows how to do. If one has ever taught a class, even for a day, one has a great deal of sympathy for the teacher's job.

Your first job then is to establish a good working relationship with your child's teacher. Occasionally chemistries don't mix, or there is a real issue about which you cannot agree, and then a good working relationship is not possible. But your first job is to attempt to establish it. Your second job is to get as much concrete information as possible about your child's progress.

How should a parent prepare for the parent-teacher conference? We would suggest that you plan it as *carefully* as you would if you were trying to get a mortgage, discussing your child's health with your physician, or buying a new car. Get a pencil and a piece of paper to make some notes before you go.

The first thing you might want to note are the comments that your child has made about his teacher or her teacher which are positive. Nothing pleases a teacher more than to be told that Bobby or Debby said such and such a nice thing about the teacher at home to their mother. So write down a few quotes of things your child has said about the teacher as a way to start off the parent conference. Be as concrete as possible. Remember what Bobby said about the field trip? What Debby said about her teacher's reaction to her map? How much fun it was for them to have the spelling bee? How nice it was when the teacher gave them a surprise party? Be specific.

The second thing to make note of is what you know about your child's study habits. How much time is your child spending on homework each night? Does your child say he has no homework on Wednesday? How much time is your child spending on TV? How sure are you about this? Do you *really* know what programs he or she is watching? What subjects does your child say are easy or difficult? Does your child say certain things are difficult, like fractions, or maps, or grammar? Does your child report that the other pupils are fun, or does he or she complain that certain children are teasing him or her? Is gym time difficult? Special class? What are the highlights of the day for your child?

Third, write the questions you want to ask the teacher for which you want some specific answers. The first question, of course, is how your child is doing in school. If you ask how he is doing and the teacher says "Oh, he's doing just fine," you may feel reassured, but you don't have much information. We would suggest that you ask for the *grade* of work that he or she is doing, and ask for it in three areas. For example, you might ask "What letter grade work would you say Bobby is doing in reading?" The teacher may not use letter grades and might demur. She might say "He is doing quite well" or "He's in the top reading group," which is helpful. But ask her to try to put it in letter grades for you, perhaps explaining that letter grades are the one thing you can really understand. Ask her to give an A, B, C, or D to Bobby or Debby's reading. Ask her to do the same thing for mathematics. Then ask her to do the same thing for his or her overall social adjustment. This will give you three grades: one for reading and one for mathematics, which are the fundamental subjects in the early grades. In addition you want to know if your youngster is helpful and cooperative in class or antagonistic or a nuisance to others.

The Conference Itself

While you are waiting, learn more about your child's classroom. Look around the room to see what books and materials are being used, and note the curriculum series (write the name of the publisher and title of the book) your child is studying. Examples of publishers of curricula are: Lippincott, Scott Foresman, Ginn (pronounced to rhyme with "kin"), Houghton Mifflin ("Ho-ton Mifflin"), Addison-Wesley, Harbrace, Silver Burdett, and Science Research Associates (SRA). Be sure to do this if it is a new school for your youngster, with a different curricular series than in the last school. Notice whose papers are displayed on the bulletin board and their content, which can give you some idea of the level of work that is regarded highly in the class. Compare these to your child's work.

Start the conference by telling the teacher some of the good things that your child has said at home about the class and about her teaching (having refreshed your memory just before the conference with those notes you have made). Everyone likes to be told that they are doing a good job. Everybody wants to be appreciated. If you consider how rare it is for teachers to hear a good word about their work, it is not very much to ask that they hear a good word from you at the beginning of the conference. This puts the teacher at ease and makes her feel that you appreciate what she is trying to do. No matter how critical you might be of some teachers, the chances are that they are trying to do the best they can in what is a very difficult and often thankless job.

After you have complemented the teacher on her work, indicate how helpful it would be to you if she could give you those letter grades. You might indicate that you don't quite understand the type of report cards with paragraph descriptions which often rate a child against his presumed ability. If the teacher says that your Bobby or Debby is doing C work or even D work, do *not* explode! Teachers are very reluctant to tell you if children are not doing well, especially in the early grades. Teachers, as a whole, are optimistic about young children. They tend to think that problems will disappear or will be outgrown, therefore they do not like to be negative about young children. On the whole this is a very sensible approach, for it often is true. On the other hand, some children who are not doing well in school need specific help, and better early than late.

The worst thing you can do is to react in an excited way about your child's lack of superior performance, suggesting to the teacher that you are the kind of parent who has unrealistic expectations for your child and is very likely pressuring the child at home. You may never pressure your child and you may be totally realistic, but it won't do for you to paint yourself into a stereotype. If the news about your child's reading or mathematics is bad, express the concern that you have in a calm way and ask the teacher how you can help your child. You might say "Of course, we don't want him to do more than he can handle, but we wonder if this is the right performance for him. What do you think?" This gives the teacher the chance to tell you whether or not she thinks that C or D work is the right level for your child's ability. If she thinks your child is capable of performing only at the C or D level, then the two of you need to talk about his ability. Ask for a good measure of ability by individual intelligence testing from the school psychologist so that you know what to expect of that child. If, on the other hand, the teacher thinks that your child could be doing B or A work and is producing only C or D, then she will be as concerned as you are, and you should work out a cooperative plan. You might ask the teacher for suggestions about how to handle the study habits at home and homework. You should come to the conference knowing how much television your child watches (which is something that few parents *really* know for sure). If your child has a television in his or her room, you probably have no way of knowing how much television is being watched. (We urge strongly against children having television sets in their own room for just this reason.) If parents want to take responsibility for monitoring how much time is being spent on television, it should be in a room where parents can check on it.

Ask the teacher what her homework expectations are. If she thinks the work should take your child an hour and a half a night and you suspect your child is spending about 30 minutes on it between TV programs, then it is *your* responsibility to do something about this problem. If your youngster is the kind who says to you each night, "I've done all my homework in study halls," then you have the problem of pinning down responsibility. This might mean a system whereby homework assignments are initialed by the teacher so that you will know how much work is actually expected. You might work out a special report form with the teacher that will let you know each day if your child has performed well at school and done his homework. There are many plans that you can work out, but the important thing is to get the teacher's cooperation and to show your willingness to assume responsibility for your part.

The parent-teacher conference is an opportunity to tell teachers about special events which might influence the behavior of your child in school, such as a recent illness or the death of a grandparent who has been particularly close to the child. It is also a time to report his or her claim to have no homework to see if this is accurate. If your youngster has a special interest in music, sports, or art, ask what the school offers in these areas.

You will be doing well to accomplish all this in ten minutes and you probably can't. If a problem does come up and you can't manage it within that amount of time, then by all means make another appointment— soon—certainly not later than next week to get at the problem. Indicate to the teacher your willingness to come (both of you, if there are two parents), to be of help, to take responsibility for studying and homework at home, and to be the kind of parent the teacher really wants to work with.

Asking About Standardized Tests

If no major problem has arisen through your review of your child's reading and mathematics and social adjustment, then you want to allow time to ask the teacher if your youngster has taken any standardized tests so far this year. You might ask: "Can you tell me if Josie has taken any standardized tests this year? I'd very much like to know how she did on them." The teacher may not have the results handy, or may not want to share them with you on the theory that you may not understand what those test scores mean—which of course you do if you have read this book! Reassure the teacher that you do understand about grade level scores and that you want some idea of how your youngster is doing against the national sample. Try to do this in as positive a way as possible. If all else fails, however, remember that you have the right to see your child's permanent record card which contains the results of all standardized tests. If the teacher finds it inconvenient to give you the results at this conference, make a point of returning to make your personal record of the test results. Be pleasant about it, but also be firm about your right to see this piece of information.

Be sure to insert in your conversation several nice things about the teacher's work with your child while you are asking for this information. She probably is afraid that in asking for information you will use it to criticize her performance. You must be very reassuring about this. It really is not her responsibility if your youngster failed to get certain skills in an earlier grade. If your youngster is in fourth grade and producing at 2.8 in reading or mathematics, and it is only November, you can hardly hold that teacher responsible for not having made up 1.2 years in the 3 months that she has been teaching your child. There is also the question of your child's natural ability in schooling, which is a key point; and the degree to which your child is applying him or herself.

Let us assume the worst for a moment. Let us assume that the teacher does have some recent standardized test scores available in her desk and has the time to tell you that your child who is now in the fourth grade in late November, which is 4.3, is actually performing, let us say, at 3.3 which is a year behind national grade level. Let us assume that this is true in both reading and mathematics. You are despondent when you hear these scores. Remember that the teacher is going to be very sensitive about those scores, feeling that they reflect on her teaching ability, which in a certain sense they do, but she cannot be held responsible for all the years that went before, or for your child's innate ability. You must immediately reassure her by saying something like this: "I am discouraged by those test scores and I know you must feel the same way, Ms. Smith. Do you think this has been going on right through the grades and we just haven't caught it, or do you think that this is something new with Freddy?" This gives the teacher a chance to tell you her view of why this has happened and does not pin her to the wall as though she were the culprit. Try to work out with your child's teacher some kind of a cooperative plan to have Freddy tested to see what his real ability for schooling is. You can also explore the possibility of some tutoring, of improving Freddy's work habits. Possibly, you may need to revise expectations because Freddy just may not be a scholar.

Ending on a Positive Note

No matter how good or bad the news about how your youngster is doing, you want to end the meeting with your child's teacher on a positive note. If it is good news, you are going to be pleased. If it is bad news, you are going to want to do something about it. You will want that teacher's cooperation, just as she wants yours. There is nothing better for a child than a school and home that work together, particularly if there is some problem in the schooling. Thank the teacher for her time and help, make another appointment if it is indicated, and tell her how much you appreciate what she is trying to do for your child.

The Teacher's Objective

From the teacher's point of view, her objective during this conference is to determine whether or not you are going to be a cooperative parent. If your child has not been performing well in school, she may have several theories why this is so. If you happen to be a divorced parent, you can expect the teacher to think that the divorce has interfered with your child's performance, which may or may not be true. If you are a working mother you can expect the same kind of attitude in many teachers. It is strange, but some teachers often have the out-of-date picture that the typical family is one with a father who works, a mother who stays home, and 2.2 children who go to school. About 40 percent of our households today are single parent households, about 50 percent of our labor force is now made up of women. The more realistic picture is of a household where mother and father both work, may or may not be married, or may or may not be divorced. Mother may head the household or there may be a father at the head of the household. These are seen as aberrations by some teachers who are likely to think that this is the source of whatever problem your child has. Perhaps the most stereotyped reaction will be to a household consisting of a mother with a child, living with a man to whom she is not married. Although the living-together-without-marriage pattern is a very common one these days, it has not yet gained acceptance in the school. Schools are very traditional in their outlook on the family, probably for good reason, so don't expect sophisticated notions about new family structures. If you happen to be living in a commune, it is probably better not to mention it at school. If you go to your parent conference wearing strange clothes or very long hair or presenting yourself in some way that could be called "hippie," you must expect the consequences. You are doing your child no favor to appear curved in a very straight environment. On the other hand, you probably do not wish to misrepresent your life at home. It is much easier to persuade a teacher that because of your interest in writing or painting or pottery that you can provide an enriched environment for your child, if you go to the school looking pretty straight. It is just a fact of school life that the more conventional you look, the more likely you are going to be accepted.

Schools judge parents by their appearance; by their dependability about coming to school when asked and coming on time; by their cooperative attitude toward the school and the teacher; and by their willingness to take responsibility for any plans that are developed. This is rather reasonable, if you look at it from the school's point of view. They want to feel that the children they teach are in the hands of responsible parents who care about them and who will take the school seriously. If your child is in a play at school, for example, you will not win points as a parent if you arrive an hour late, or fail to show up. By all means, arrive on time! It is probably unwise to say that Sally does her homework "during cocktail hour." It may be true, but it gives a rather undesirable impression about home life. This does not mean that you need to misrepresent things at home. But it does mean that you should choose your descriptors carefully in terms of how it will appear to another person. You would feel the same way if you were teaching a class. You would look for parents who seem to be responsible, concerned, and dependable. You would be concerned if you thought this child went home to a family that was almost never home; one where the father was there and then he wasn't there; or where the mother did not supervise the homework or the children; or where there was a lot of "carrying on." The teacher looks upon her pupils partly as her own children and is generally concerned for them.

Following the Conference

Now the parent-teacher conference is over and you come home. Your child is going to ask you about what the teacher said. What do you answer? First, you say how much you enjoyed meeting Ms. so and so. If this is a teacher whom your child really dislikes, your child will groan, but it is still important to indicate that you respect the teacher. We do not hold with criticizing teachers in front of your children unless a strong case of injustice exists. Keep your reservations to yourself after this one exposure, unless you feel there is a real case of mistreatment or misteaching going on. Then proceed to tell your child what was said in the parent-teacher conference. Our view is that honesty is almost always the best policy. We would suggest telling your child everything that you can remember, including reading from your notes about his or her progress, his or her test results, his or her performance in reading, mathematics, and social adjustment. The more that you and the teacher and your child share the same information, the better off you are. It is always possible that the teacher has shared some information with you that you may not think is wise to share with your child at just this moment. The teacher might have indicated that she thinks your child's friendship with another child is not helping either of them in mathematics, in fact they are fooling around in mathematics class. You might decide to tell your child just that, or you might decide you wanted more information about the other youngster, or wanted a better time to handle it.

In general we subscribe to the idea that your child should know as much as possible about his performance, just as you should. If you are planning to have another appointment with the teacher, tell your youngster that you are going and why you are going. If, as a result of the

parent-teacher conference, you are concerned about your child's progress, tell him or her just that and why you are concerned. You might say "Yes, I was concerned to hear that you're doing C and D work in mathematics, and I think we owe it to you to find out why this is so. One thing we are going to do is to find out how naturally good you are at mathematics first, so that your father and I (assuming the father is in the picture) won't be expecting too much from you. That is why I am making an appointment for you to see the psychologist next week to get a test on your mathematics ability." Or if you found a reading problem, you might say, "She said you were doing very well in mathematics and in science, but she felt that you were a bit behind in your reading. I asked her for your reading scores and find that you are about a year behind in reading. I think this is something that we need to get onto right away, George, because I don't want you to go through school with difficulties in reading. I know that would be very hard on you. I think what we ought to do is make an appointment to test your reading and see if there is some place that could give us some help. I'll be going to school next week to make the appointment."

If you have been fortunate to hear a very good report about your child, then you might say, "I was very pleased to meet her and she is *so* pleased with your work at school! She told me that you're doing B work in reading and A work in mathematics and science. I also saw your test scores and you are doing a little bit above grade level in reading and mathematics. I think that is just wonderful and I know your Dad will be pleased (if Dad is in the picture and did not attend the conference) when I tell him. I think maybe we should make a special supper tonight or tomorrow night to celebrate. What would you like to have?" Perhaps you might find a better reward than the special supper, but children often like the idea that they can order their very own favorite foods. The point is to make something *important* of the occasion, because progress in school is the most important thing that your child is likely to do for a number of years. It is not very rewarding for a child to do well in school, and to hear nothing about it when the parent comes home. It suggests an attitude of "we expect you to do well, so when you do well we don't say anything." There is nothing more disheartening than effort that goes unrewarded. Make a fuss over your youngsters' progress and let them know that it matters to you!

Often parents say nothing complimentary about their child's school progress because they think a child should develop on their own and that school progress is just to be expected. Our view is—what a mistaken notion! Parents not only should be interested and concerned about their child's school progress, but should make as much over it as they do over their own work. *Going to school is a child's work.* When mother or father get a promotion or raise or new assignment, it is a time for great celebration. In school, the time to celebrate is when your youngster is found to be doing well. So celebrate!

How to Read Achievement Test Scores and Reports

During the parent-teacher conference, you are likely to find out the results your child has received on standardized tests which have been administered throughout the school system. Since standardized achievement tests are the most important tests administered in school, we will discuss how to read achievement test scores and reports, including the most frequently used terms you are likely to encounter.

What Is a Standardized Test?

The term "standardized" refers to the standard or uniform conditions under which a test was developed and is to be administered. Tests of reading achievement, aptitude, and intelligence are all examples of standardized tests. In standardizing a test, many factors are taken into account. Age, sex, race, region of the country, rural and urban areas, and the varying backgrounds of children in the original sample must all be considered when a publisher develops a standardized test to make sure that, when the test is used in schools across the country, the results are representative of the performance of many different children. Black children, white children, city children, children from rural settings, children from working-class homes, children from poor families, and children from rich families must all be included. So "standardized" means first that a representative sample of children was used on which to base the results of the test.

Standardized also implies that the *same* set of instructions must be given to all children without changes in wording by the teacher. The same

standardized procedures must be used in the presentation of materials and the same time limits imposed on all children taking the test. Each child is tested using uniform (standardized) procedures so that all children have had the same opportunity on that test. The conditions under which the test was developed are presented in the technical portions of most test manuals which should be available to teachers and other test administrators.

Standardized achievement tests measure the child's present level of knowledge in the subject areas taught. Children in different classes and schools across the country have teachers who present learning material in very different ways, and who expect different levels of performance from their children. We have all experienced easy teachers and hard teachers. Sometimes it is useful, however, to find out how children fare when compared with other children of the same age or grade in the same subject matter area. Standardized achievement tests help answer questions of this sort. They also help teachers and schools locate areas of curriculum that need particular work, and to know when they have made important gains in teaching certain subjects. They help school systems evaluate whether an innovative program is working or whether it is more effective with some pupils than others.

No test should be used to imply that all children must function in the same way. They cannot. The developers of standardized tests do not intend to imply that children must conform to a uniform goal. A problem arises when test results are misused to suggest each child should reach the same level. It is the responsibility of the school to ensure that such misuse of information does not occur.

"Standardization" then refers specifically to two important conditions:

1. Conditions under which the test was developed resulting in a set of standards of performance that represent a wide sample of children
2. Conditions under which the test is administered, resulting in a uniform way to give the test so that all children have the same chance

How Most Achievement Tests Are Given, Scored, Reported, and Recorded

In thousands of public and private schools across the United States, pupils take standardized achievement tests each year which are administered to the class as a whole by the teacher, and generally sent to the test publisher for machine scoring. The tests themselves are not usually returned, but the results are. The results come in a variety of forms. One form reports scores for each pupil with an analysis of each item passed or failed; another reports scores alphabetically by class; another compares pupils to other classes in the same building or school district; another form compares achievement test scores with IQ scores; another explains each pupil's score in a narrative form for parents and teachers; still another provides criterion-referenced information which reports a child's progress in each specific educational skill, such as a child's skill in mathematical operations, or in spelling, or in reading tables and graphs. Each form costs the school money. The more detailed and the more it explains, the more each form costs.

A common form of achievement test reporting that parents are likely to encounter is the economical press-on label of results, a label which is literally pressed onto the pupil's permanent record. These press-on labels are extremely difficult for anyone to read, because too much information is compressed into a small label with a perceptually confusing layout.

Decoding Test Report Language

In order to understand what is printed on this label, parents need to be familiar with the terms that are currently used and their abbreviations.

Grade Equivalent Score = GE, or Natl. (National) GE[1]

Most test scores report a pupil's results in terms of a grade equivalent, because progress in U.S. schools is measured by the grade a pupil is in, not by his age. A third grade class can contain children who have just become eight or are still seven, as well as nine and ten year olds. So the grade is the unit by which we tend to measure school progress.

Grade equivalent means that the school year has been divided into its 10 months (September to June = 10 months) so that we can express where a child is in terms of grade + number of months in that grade. If a child took a test in late November in third grade, his grade placement at time of testing would be third grade and three months (September, October, and November), expressed as 3.3 grade placement (see Appendix C, "Interpreting Grade Equivalent Scores"). If that child is progressing at an average pace, he or she will score *around* 3.3 in the overall test scores. That overall score is expressed as a *grade equivalent* score, meaning that this performance is what average pupils did when they were at the third grade, three months level. Each child then is compared to what average children do at each grade and at each month in that grade. Look for how much below, or how much above, your child's score is compared to your child's actual grade placement. If your child was at 4.2 when tested, then you hope to see a GE score that is *around* that level, for example 3.8 to 4.4.

[1]Test report language varies in using capitals, punctuation, and abbreviations, following computer convenience rather than English grammar.

Parents need to be very careful about interpreting grade equivalent scores, especially when they are high. A student in fifth grade, for example, can receive a grade equivalent score that says "7.1," which implies that this student can read at a seventh grade, first month level of reading. This child is reading well for a fifth grader, and on the test has scored at what the test norms call 7.1. But this does not mean this child could walk into a seventh grade class in September and read on the same level as that class. These grade equivalent scores, especially the high ones, have to be taken as a number indicating high performance, but not as a measure of true reading ability. Likewise, another fifth grader who receives a grade equivalent score of 2.5 in reading does not read like the average second grader at the middle of the year. Rather, the fifth grader is experiencing considerable difficulty.

This is why we prefer that parents ask for percentile scores (and wish schools would use them uniformly). Percentile scores tell you the comparative performance of your child against other children, not against an arbitrary grade progress standard.

National Percentile Score or Rank = PR (Percentile Rank)

The second way a pupil's performance is reported is as a national percentile. A percentile score (or rank) shows where a pupil stands in relation to some particular group, and is expressed in a percentile score ranging from a low of 1 to a high of 99. A percentile score is like a ladder with 99 rungs. If a pupil has a percentile score of 10, that means he or she scored better than the 9 percentile ranks (or rungs) below 10, and not as well as the 89 (99–10) who are above. A percentile score of 50 is exactly at the middle of the ladder—½ are above, ½ are below. A percentile score of 75 means the pupil scored better than the 74 percentile ranks below his or her score, and not as well as the 24 (99–75) who were above.

If student scores at:	*The score means:*
The 10th percentile	10 percent of the original test sample performed *below* this student
The 25th percentile	25 percent of the original test sample performed *below* this student
The 50th percentile	50 percent of the original test sample performed *below* this student
The 75th percentile	75 percent of the original test sample performed *below* this student
The 95th percentile	95 percent of the original test sample performed *below* this student

We could say that a percentile rank of 90 would suggest excellent understanding of the subject matter being tested. Percentiles can be interpreted in the following way:[2]

90–99   excellent understanding
70–89   good understanding
60–69   somewhat above average understanding
40–59   average understanding
30–39   somewhat below average understanding
10–29   difficulty encountered
 1–9   greater difficulty encountered

It is important to note that percentile scores are *not* the familiar percent scores. A percent is a raw score which is expressed in terms of the percentage of items answered correctly.

Since no test is a perfect measure of a child's achievement, many schools prefer to report *percentile bands*, which give the top and bottom of the range in which the score fell. The advantage of percentile bands is that they help the teacher and parent focus on the *range* in which the child's scores are likely to occur on each subtest, indicating when differences in scores between subtests are meaningful. Percentile bands take into account that if a child were to take the same test over and over again, that his or her test score would vary somewhere within the band.

There is a special characteristic about percentiles that is important to understand. For the child who scores very poorly at the lst or 5th percentile, or extremely well at the 95th or 99th percentile, a large change in score results in a *small* change in percentile. But for the child who scores near the middle of the group, a small change in score, even 2 or 3 points, can result in a *large* change in percentile.

Therefore, the difference between a percentile of 85 and 92 should be considered a meaningful difference. But the difference between a percentile of 51 and 55 would not be meaningful.

Despite this drawback, percentiles are easier to compare from test to test than are grade equivalent scores and *should be requested by parents*.

Some hints that might help you interpret the meaning of percentiles include:

When comparing a child's performance from one subject area to another, a percentile difference of 10 points may suggest areas of relative strength or weakness; a percentile difference of 20 or more points, however, may suggest an area where the child may need some special work or further diagnostic testing, or it may suggest an area of particular strength.

When comparing a child's performance in the same subject area over time, small changes in percentile at the extreme ends (above 90th

[2]See NCME *Measurement News*, April 1974, vol. 14, no. 2, p. 5.

percentile or below 10th percentile), may indicate important changes in the child's performance. The changes in score to move from a percentile rank of 91 to 95 are much greater than to move from 51 to 55.

For percentiles in the normal range of 30 to 70, a change from 51 to 45 or from 58 to 63 may simply mean the child answered one or two more questions correctly or incorrectly. The child's standing in comparison to other children taking the test is more or less the same.

If your child is attending an independent school, be *sure* to ask the teacher for *independent school percentiles* since national percentiles may present a different picture of your child's performance. For example, a child might receive a percentile rank of 85 when compared to national norms, and a percentile rank of 55 when compared to independent school norms.

National percentile ranks (Natl. PR) mean just what they say, namely, that the percentile ranks referred to on the test scores are based on a national sample of pupils who took the test, so that each pupil is being compared to national percentiles, not just local ones. National percentiles tell us how a pupil does compared to a sample of pupils across the *whole* United States, which is a broader and more stable comparison than a local sample.

Local Norms

Often it is helpful to interpret the meaning of scores on a test on a local basis in terms of how other children in the same community perform. For example, on tests of reading achievement, it might be important to learn how a child performs in relationship to other children in the same grade in the same school system or in the same type of reading program. Thus many communities develop local norms over time so that appropriate levels of expectation can be determined and teaching programs planned. For many tests, norms have been developed for special populations, such as children attending private schools, or the hearing or visually impaired.

Stanines

The third way scores are reported is in "stanines." Stanine scores range from a low of 1 to a high of 9, and are based on standard scores. Standard scores are a way of converting a score on any test into a common language. A standard score represents both the degree of alikeness (the average) of all scores and the degree of difference (variation). Standard scores are expressed in two numbers. When computers became popular, it was handy to use only one column (0–9) of a standard punchcard to report a score, so stanines (pronounced stay-nines) were invented to report a score in only one number. Stanine scores range from 1 to 9, as we said above, with the average set at 5.[3] (See Appendix F, "Converting Stanines to Percentiles.")

So here are those abbreviations again:

GE = grade equivalent, from 1.1 (first grade first month) to 12.9 (twelfth grade, ninth month)

PR = percentile rank from 1 (low) to 99 (high)

NATL = national

LOC = local

STANINE = stanines range from 1 (low) to 9 (high)

In addition to these three types of scores—grade equivalents, percentiles, and stanines—some reports will show two sets of comparisons. One comparison is to "PS" norms, which means public school norms; and the other is "IS" norms, which means independent school norms. Parents whose children are in independent (private) schools will want to make *sure* they apply the IS norms against their children's test results, if they want to know how well their children are achieving as compared to other private school pupils.

PS = public school norms

IS = independent (private) school norms

When Are Achievement Tests Given?

School systems vary in the time at which they test. Most wait until children are back in school for two months or more, so the children can rehearse what they forgot over the summer, get used to their new teacher, and settle into the classroom routine. Achievement testing usually does not start before October. Many schools prefer to test at the midpoint, in January or February, so that this year's teacher can have the benefit of the test results with which to plan instruction for each child for the second semester. Other schools prefer to carry out their achievement testing toward the end of the year, March through May, so they can tell how much has been learned that year.

Your child will tell you when the tests have been taken. What you want to know is when they *will* be taken, so you can make sure your child goes to school rested, motivated to do well, with current work assignments completed.

Ask the teacher or principal which achievement tests are given in your child's grade, and when they are given. Write down the name of the tests and the dates of the test weeks. Put them on your calendar with a note and make sure your child has a restful weekend before they start.

[3]Cronbach, L. J. *Essentials of Psychological Testing* (3rd ed.), New York: Harper & Row, 1970.

The most commonly given achievement tests in grades 1–12 are the Iowa, Stanford, Metropolitan, SRA, and California tests. These tests are named for the universities (Iowa, Stanford) where they were developed, or in the area where they first were used. Each series has different forms of each test suitable for a cluster of grades. For example, Forms 7 and 8 of the Iowa test are designed for grades 3–9, with six *levels* within each form to cover the ability of children in grades 3–9. Usually there are two forms of each test so that if a child has taken one form recently, another equivalent form is available. When you take notes on your child's achievement test scores be sure to write down these five basic items of information:

1. The name of the test
2. When given
3. Form given
4. Level given
5. Record the scores themselves

Test scores mean nothing without the name of the test, when it was given, the form, and the level administered. The two most important pieces of information are the name of the test and when it was given. The timing of a test is crucial because *all school learning is based on time.* Sound crazy? Not if you stop to think that we expect older children to know more than younger children—fourth graders to read better than second graders. That is because our school system, like most school systems, assumes that the longer you go to school (= time) the more you know. All an achievement test can tell us (even if the test were perfect) is how much this pupil knows, at *this point in time.* So always record when the test was given. In this way, you (and anyone you consult) can compute the grade equivalent of your child at time of testing. If the test were given in March of fifth grade, we will know that the child's grade placement at time of testing was 5.7. Here is a handy table for computing grade placement. (For future reference, consult Appendix B, Interpreting Grade Equivalent Scores.)

Table 1
COMPUTING GRADE PLACEMENT

grade = grade your child is in month of year	decimal equivalent
September	= .1
October	= .2
November	= .3
December	= .4
January	= .5
February	= .6
March	= .7
April	= .8
May	= .9

How to Read Achievement Test Scores

If shown your child's permanent record with its press-on labels of achievement test scores, the information may look like this:

XYZ TEST

School: Central
Student: John Doe   grade: 6th   Level: 12   Form: 7
Date tested: 2/80

Translation.   This part is fairly straightforward. John Doe attends Central School, is in the sixth grade, took level 12 Form 7 of this XYZ test on 2/80, or February 1980.

Now here comes the hard part. It may look like this:

V	R	L-1	L-2	L-3	L-4	L-TOT	W-1	W-2	W-TOT
Vocab	Readg	Splg	Captn	Puntn	Usage	Lang	Vis M	Ref M	Wd St
GE PR	GE PR	GE PR	GE PR	GE PR	GE PR	GE PR	GE PR	GE PR	GE PR
82 82	90 91	63 47	90 85	83 79	63 47	75 68	67 54	85 86	76 74

Translation.   Let us translate each of these blocks above into comprehensible English. Let us start at the left.

    V = vocabulary subtest
    GE = grade equivalent

John Doe took this test in February 1980 when he was in the sixth grade, so John's grade placement, at time of testing, was 6.6 (sixth grade, sixth month) so we will compare his GE scores to his GE placement of 6.6.

On vocabulary (V or vocab) John received a grade equivalent score of 82 (eighth grade, second month), which means John is ahead of his current grade placement by the difference between his actual grade placement and his achieved score, or 6.6 compared to 82 (read 8.2—test reports omit the decimal to save space!). John is achieving 8.2 over 6.6, 1.5 grade equivalent years above his placement in vocabulary—or, he is achieving about a year and one-half above his current grade placement.

This 1.5 year achievement above his grade placement puts John at the 82nd percentile (PR = percentile rank) which means that John is doing better in vocabulary than 81 percent of the sample that took this test in his grade, and less well than (99–82) 17 percentile ranks above him.

This all adds up to a very creditable performance in vocabulary for John Doe.

Now let's tackle those other symbols!

    R = reading

John got 9.0 (grade equivalent of ninth grade, 0 month in reading) which put him at the 91st percentile. John is obviously an excellent reader. His reading score is about three grades above his grade placement of 6.6, and even a better measure, John scores at the 91st percentile of other sixth graders in reading. That is a strong reading performance!

    L-1 = first language arts subtest, of which there are four
Splg = spelling
  GE = 63, PR = 47

John is about at his grade placement (6.6) in spelling, and at the 47th percentile, which is close to the average.

    L-2 = second language arts subtest, of which there are four
Captn = capitalization
  GE = 90, PR = 85

A fine performance in capitalization. John is at the ninth grade, 0 month in capitalization, about three years above his grade placement of 6.3. The percentile rank of 85 is also high.

    L-3 = third language arts subtest, of which there are four.
Puntn = punctuation
  GE = 83, PR = 79

In this third language subtest, on punctuation, John received an 8.3 GE, which is almost two years above his actual grade placement of 6.6, and puts him at the 79th percentile, which is also a high percentile (higher than 78 lower rungs on the ladder).

    L-4 = fourth language subtest
Usage = a subtest on language usage
  GE = 63, PR = 47

On this subtest of language usage, John is about at his grade placement and at the middle (47) of the percentile rank.

L-TOT = total language score
  Lang = language, covering all four language subtests
    GE = 75, PR = 68

This gives us the average language score for John. He was high in capitalization; above average in punctuation; and about average in spelling and language usage. All of these four subtests are represented in the total language score (L-TOT = language total) where John scored 7.5 in grade equivalent (GE) which is about one year above his grade placement; and at the 68th percentile, which is also above the middle (50th) percentile rank. So John has done quite well in his language subtest.

    W-1 = work-study subtest number one
Vis M = visual materials (map reading, reading graphs and tables)
  GE = 67, PR = 54

This first subtest on work-study skills measures the skill of reading maps, which students do in the study of history; and reading of graphs and tables, which is needed in social studies, in science, and in mathematics. John is at his grade placement in these skills, scoring 67, a 6.7 grade equivalent compared to 6.6 for his actual grade placement; and at the 54th percentile which is just about average.

> W-2 = the second work-study subtest
> Ref M = reference materials
> GE = 85, PR = 86

This second subtest on work-study skills tests a number of skills needed for using reference materials, such as the ability to use an index correctly; using a dictionary and an encyclopedia; and alphabetizing correctly. On this subtest John has done quite well, scoring 85, or 8.5 GE which is about two years ahead of his grade placement, putting him at the 86th percentile.

> W-TOT = total
> Wk St = work-study skills
> GE = 76   PR = 74

Overall, on work-study skills John is about a year ahead (7.6 compared to 6.6) and ranks at the 74th percentile which is almost at the upper quartile. (The upper quartile is from the 75th to the 99th percentile; the lower quartile would be from the 25th percentile to the 1st percentile; the two middle quartiles would be from the 26th to the 50th and from the 51st to the 75th percentile. Sometimes it is easier to divide the percentile ranks into quartiles, as one-fourth, so we can focus on the overall performance and not get lost in the details of each percentile.)

What Do These Scores Really Mean?

A word now is in order about how meaningful each of these scores are. As a parent, should you be upset if your child's grade placement is 6.6, like our mythical John Doe above, and he scores 6.5, or 6.4, or 6.3, on any of these subtests? No one subtest score should be considered noteworthy by itself, if it falls within six months (plus or minus) of the child's grade placement. In the case of John Doe, one subtest score at 6.0 should not be cause for alarm. Each of these subtests is short, because of the pressure of time, and a student may misread one or two questions, or lose his or her place on the answer sheet, or even skip a question or two inadvertently. Any of these slips can affect a subtest score.

So the first rule is not to take any one subtest score as proof, but to look at the overall pattern of subtest scores. Pay *special* attention to reading and vocabulary because they are basic skills which are practiced and taught a great deal in the curriculum. Look at the *total* language score and the *total* word-study score before you examine the individual subtests. In this way, you can get an overall picture of your child's performance which will tell you if the performance is near grade placement, below, or above. Look for differences of a year or more on the subtests to suggest strengths and weaknesses. John Doe was very high in vocabulary and reading, two strong indications of school progress. His spelling was down about two years, as was language usage, suggesting he needs more work in these two areas. But his overall performance shows percentiles of 82 in vocabulary, a 91 in reading, 68 in total language arts, and 74 in work-study skills—a very creditable performance indeed.

What Is Wrong with Grade Equivalent Scores?

The grade equivalent scores that we discussed above are based on national averages. That means that very above average schools and below average schools are all lumped together to make up an expected standard of school progress. The standard that usually is applied is the grade equivalent score.

The grade equivalent score is, in the opinion of many school measurement experts, one of the poorest measures we could use. Why? Because a grade equivalent score sounds as though all children should be at a certain point of knowledge when they are at a certain point in the grade. A grade equivalent score of 3.4 when a child's placement is third grade, fourth month, seems to say that a child is exactly right—3.4 at 3.4. But if a child gets 3.3, he or she is below grade placement! If we arranged all third grade children who took this test in a row, from highest score to lowest score, roughly half would be above their grade placement and roughly half would be below. The grade equivalent standard implies that 50 percent of the children are not doing well when, in fact, they are just doing what human beings do in most things—they are falling into a distribution where most are in the middle, and few are at the top and bottom—the normal curve.

One of the larger mistakes in public education may be that it adapted a poor measure of progress in the grade equivalent scores. Every time a school, especially an inner city or isolated rural school, reports its test scores in terms of grade equivalents, the media picks up that pupils "scored below grade." It would be much more informative if the results were given in percentiles.

Suppose the Child Attends a Below Average School

What does a parent do if his or her child is in a school where the average scores are "below grade level," as is true in many schools in the inner core of our largest cities? The first thing is to ask for the school system or district's results, as a whole, and then to have your child's scores compared to the district's scores. For example, let's move our John Doe into an inner city school in one of our largest cities. John Doe is still in the sixth grade, sixth month, so his grade placement is still 6.6. His achievement test scores for reading are 4.8, for vocabulary 4.9; for total language arts 3.9; for work-study skills 3.7. What do these scores mean? They mean that John City Doe is behind in his school achievement as measured by these tests. But John City Doe may be trying very hard, and doing well in comparison to the rest of his classmates in his school. To find out how John is doing in comparison to other pupils in the same school environment, his parents need to ask for his school *district's* test results and his school *building's* test results. All city school districts should have district-wide scores and school building scores. Ask for them, and ask to have your child's scores compared to them. If we do that for John City Doe, we may find that although John's scores are behind the national average, he is doing well in comparison to his district and building. For example, John City Doe scored 4.8 in reading, but we may find that his grade (6th) in his district scored 4.2 in reading, so John is well ahead of his classmates in his district. Be sure to ask for percentile scores!

There are many reasons given as to why pupils in inner city schools and in poorer rural areas score lower than the national average. Among the reasons that have been given are inadequate teaching; lack of pupil motivation; insufficient school resources; poor discipline; lack of parental instruction; racism; pupils' inadequate nutrition; pollution; the culture of poverty; and a general feeling of despair in these schools. At the present time, no clear cause-and-effect has been demonstrated to explain these lower scores.

A parent is well advised to compare his or her child's scores against his or her school district and building before coming to any judgment about how well or how poorly that child is performing. A child can be behind the national average and still be near the top of his or her grade for the district. If so, that child is doing a good job in that school.

What Other Scores Am I Likely to See?

The scores we have discussed above refer to frequently used achievement test programs. Following are some other test scores, most of which use the same type of abbreviation and layout:

Name: Doe, Jane
Grade: 04, test date 10/80
Age: 9–10
Lvl: Pri II FM A Natl—4.2

Score type	Vocab.	Reading Compre- hension	Word Study Skill	Math Concepts	Math Compu- tation	Math Applica- tion
GE	4.2	5.4	3.5	6.0	4.5	4.7
Natl. PR-S	50-5	84-7	49-5	92-8	72-6	68-6
Loc. PR-S	56-5	88-7	45-5	98-9	79-7	74-6

We read this one as we did the last, translating from the left as we go. Jane Doe, it says, is in the 4th grade ("04), tested in 10/80 (October 1980) which puts her in the second month of her fourth grade, a 4.2 grade placement for "natl. norms," as it says in the fourth line, beginning "Lv1." She is aged 9 years, 10 months at the time of testing, when she took this particular test, the level of which was Primary II, Form A.

Here is the code about what these next abbreviations mean:

GE = grade equivalent
Natl PR-S = national percentile and stanine
Loc PR-S = local percentile and stanine

Let us take each set of scores, by column, and translate to see how Jane Doe is doing. Jane's grade placement is 4.2, we will remember, so we will look for scores around that figure, and pay even more attention to the percentiles.

Vocabulary

Jane has 4.2 in her grade equivalent (GE) score in reading, which is exactly where she is in grade placement—fourth grade, and second (October) month. Her national percentile (Natl PR) is 50, right smack at the middle, and her national stanine (S) is 5. So her reading is exactly average, nationally, in these measures. On local percentiles and stanines (Loc PR-S) which is for her school district, she is at the 56th percentile and the same 5th stanine. What this means is that Jane's school district is a little bit below the national average because Jane's reading score is at the 50th percentile, nationally, but at the 56th locally, showing that Jane is doing a little bit better compared to her school district than she is nationally.

Reading Comprehension

These scores are read exactly the same way. Jane has 5.4 in grade equivalency score (GE) in reading comprehension, which puts her at the 84th percentile nationally (Natl PR) and at the 7th national stanine (S). This is a fine performance and this puts Jane at the 88th percentile locally (Loc PR) in her own district and at the 7th stanine locally (S).

Word-study Skills

In this section, Jane does less well, with 3.5 grade equivalency score (GE), which puts her at the 49th national percentile and the 5th stanine (Natl PR-S) and at the 45th local percentile (usually the school district is the local comparison) and at the 5th local stanine (Loc PR-S).

Math Concepts

This is Jane's strongest area. She obtains 6.0 grade equivalent scores (GE) in math concepts, placing her at the 92nd national percentile and at the 8th national stanine (Natl PR-S); and at the 98th local percentile and the 9th local stanine (Loc PR-S). These are excellent scores, near the top of the national percentiles in "math concepts," which tests mathematical operations, geometry, measurement, notation, and numeration at this level of the test.

Math Computation

At this level, "math computation" tests basic facts—the sort of mathematics knowledge we all remember, such as the times tables, how to do long division, how to add, and how to subtract. Jane is at 4.5 grade equivalency; at the 72nd national percentile and 6th national stanine; and at the 79th local percentile and the 7th local stanine. Her performance is less good in computation than it is in math concepts. One would think that Jane could improve her computation score by practicing more, either with flash cards or on a computer, where programs are now available that offer practice in computation.

Math Application

This subtest asks students to apply mathematics to everyday problems, (what we used to know as word problems but applied to real-life situations). Here Jane does about as well as she did on "math computation," with a grade equivalency score (GE) of 4.7. But this time we note that a slightly higher GE score of 4.7, compared to 4.5 in math computation, puts Jane at a slightly lower national (68) and local (74) percentiles. How can this be? Two explanations, at least are possible. The first is that this particular subtest was composed of relatively easy items, so more students got more of them right, thus making it harder to get high percentile rankings. The other possibility is that the material covered by the test happens to be taught more intensively in the schools than is math computation and that therefore pupils were more practiced for the items on this subtest, consequently performed better as a group, thereby making it harder to get the higher percentiles.

The differences in percentiles are small between "math computation" and "math application" so we do not need to concern ourselves with the differences. Jane scored at the 68th percentile nationally and at the 6th national stanine; at the local level, she scored at the 74th percentile and the 6th stanine.

Overall Performance

Jane is doing very well in reading comprehension and math concepts; well in math computation and application; average in vocabulary; and about average in work-study skills.

Other Symbols and Abbreviations

In addition to the common ones we have described so far, you may encounter the following abbreviations in achievement test scores, listed here with their translations.

No Rt = number right = number of items the student answered correctly

No Pos = number possible = number of all possible items which student could have answered correctly

Spelling = test results of the ability to spell correctly

Social science = test results in elementary social science and history

Science = test results in elementary science

Listening comprehension = test results in the ability to listen and comprehend what is spoken

V Reas = verbal reasoning

N Abil = numerical ability

A Reas = arithmetic reasoning

M Reas = mechanical reasoning

Sp Rel = spatial relations

DAT = Differential Aptitude Tests, given usually in the eighth or ninth grade

What Do Early Test Scores Predict About Later Performance?

Let us take a look at one student's test record from first grade through twelfth grade to see how well or poorly these early tests predict later high school scores. This predictive value is important. Many parents want advance estimates about their child's future performance on high school tests that influence entrance into college. These tests, called SAT (Scholastic Achievement Test) and the College Board examinations in specific subjects (sciences, languages, etc.) play an important role in the decision to admit a student to a particular college. They become very important in a student's life in grades eleven and twelve.

Can we predict from test scores in the early grades how a student is likely to perform in high school? The answer is a qualified "yes" for a large number of students, with the reservation that any one prediction for any one student is a chancy business. It is always much more reliable to predict group behavior than individual behavior. If we were to give a party for 25 fourth graders, we could predict that most of them will choose chocolate or vanilla ice cream. But if we were to try to predict what flavor Tom would like, we might be entirely wrong, because Tom is an individual who hates chocolate and vanilla, but loves banana.

If we selected 50 classes of first graders at random across the United States (which would add up to 50 × 25 average students per class, or 1250 students) and if we looked at their first grade test scores in reading, we could make a moderately reliable prediction about the group's average test score in eleventh grade; and through a statistical technique, we could even make a prediction about each member of that group, so that an overall accuracy for each of the 1250 students would be above chance. But we still could be wrong about a number of individuals, especially those at the very high and very low end of the scores. The higher the score, or the lower the score, the less reliable it is. The more extreme the score, the more likely that chance is at work.

Let us look at one student's scores over time to see what a long-range view shows us. We will call the student Max. These are actual scores for a student from first through twelfth grade.

Max entered the district in kindergarten when he had no tests. In first grade, in October, he received a reading readiness test which purports to predict how easily a child will learn to read. Max received a national percentile score of 93, which is very high and suggests Max should be a strong and early reader.

But in grade two we see "Lorge-Thorndike, grade two, DIQ-101." Translated that means that Max, on the Lorge-Thorndike test, which is a group test, received a developmental IQ of 101. That puts Max at about exactly the average of IQ, at the 50th percentile, which is considerably lower than the 93rd percentile we saw in the first grade. What happened? Why the difference?

The rules in evaluating test scores are:

1. *The more extreme the score, the less reliable (repeatable) it is.* Max's score in the 93rd percentile was very high, and therefore less likely to be reliable (repeated exactly).

The second rule in evaluating test scores is:

2. *The younger the age of testing, the less reliable the score.* If you think about this second rule a minute, it will make a lot of sense to you. It is part of a more general rule which is the younger the child, the more changeable the child is. It is foolhardy to predict a two year old will be a scientist because the child likes to peer at bugs at age two. Inclinations that show at five or six years may increase, or decrease, as the years go by. But when a child reaches an older age, we can make more reliable statements about enduring characteristics.

And so it is with test scores. A score at 4 or 5 years is not a reliable predictor of performance at 10 or 12, not only because the child is young, but because a lot of changes occur between age 4 and age 10—a lot, as any parent knows.

Max, who tested in the very high range in first grade may have been ahead of his contemporaries in reading readiness because he just happened to grow faster, at that age, in these abilities; or perhaps he came from a home where reading was emphasized, where he was read to a great deal, and where vocabulary was taught. By grade two, these advantages appear to have evened out, and now we have Max at the average, or 50th percentile of IQ. From this we would predict an average test performance in the future. But what actually happened?

The next test results come in grade five, when Max receives another form of Lorge-Thorndike. On this Max scores at the 93rd percentile in the verbal section, and at the 55th percentile in the nonverbal section, with a total IQ of 113. This puts him right between his first and second grade scores, so now we see Max as above average in school ability. Why was his second grade score low? Was he sick that day, or not attending to the test?

In fifth grade, Max was given the Iowa test of Basic Skills, one of the more widely used achievement tests, so now we have a chance to see how well he is achieving in school, as compared to the measures of potential ability which the IQ is thought to represent. Max's performance is excellent. He receives total scores between the 89th and 97th percentiles, with an average performance at the 94th percentile. This high performance in achievement suggests that this readiness test at the 93rd percentile in first grade was *very* predictive of Max's performance 4 years later! More and more, that second grade IQ score of 101 looks out of line, and an unrepresentative performance. On any test, especially one taken on one day for only 30 to 40 minutes, a young child can be off his or her performance, due to an unrecognized illness, missing directions, putting answers in the wrong places, or missing critical weeks of school when certain content was taught. (It would be wise to check Max's attendance record for grade two to see if he was absent prior to the test.)

In the fall of sixth grade, Max took his statewide (regional) test in mathematics, when he scored at the 85th percentile overall, a very creditable performance. This test result is consistent with the previous higher scores, so we predict Max will be a strong mathematics student.

In grade six, Max also received the Pimsleur language test, which attempts to assess a student's aptitude for learning foreign languages. This usually is given in sixth grade to help a student decide about taking a foreign language in seventh grade at the beginning of junior high school. Max's total percentile score was at the 94th percentile, suggesting Max would be an excellent foreign language student.

Now Max enters seventh grade and junior high school, where he takes the DAT (Differential Aptitude Test). The purpose of the DAT is to assess a student's aptitude in several abilities required in high school work. The abilities tested are: verbal reasoning (V Reas); numerical ability (N Abil); arithmetic reasoning (A Reas); clerical speed and accuracy (Cl S + A); mechanical reasoning (M Reas); spatial relations (Sp Rel); and language abilities (Lang 1 & 2). The most predictive score in the DAT is thought to be the combination of VR and NA (verbal reasoning and numerical ability) because these two abilities are fundamental to success in most high school course work, and even college work. (These two scores are similar to the SAT score on verbal and mathematics, which we will discuss below.)

Max's combination percentile on VR and NA is the 75th percentile, a strong showing but not as high as some of his earlier achievement tests.

There are no test scores for Max until the fall of his eleventh grade, or junior year, when he takes the PSAT, the Preliminary Scholastic Aptitude Test. On this he receives a verbal score of 45 and a mathematics score of 56, both very creditable scores. (Read 450 for 45; 560 for 56.)

Max takes the SAT itself in October of twelfth grade, and this time scores 49 verbal, 54 mathematics, not really a change in score. In December of twelfth grade, Max retakes the SAT, and improves his score slightly by receiving a 52 verbal and 54 mathematics score, both good scores. A combined score on the SAT of 52 and 54 means 520 + 540 = 1060, which puts Max well above the average SAT total of 740 required for public 4-year colleges, and the 754 required for private 4-year colleges, as shown in Appendix G, Table 2, p. 178.

That brings us to the end of the test score saga for Max, who proved to be of high tested ability throughout his school years, with the exception of that odd score on the Lorge-Thorndike in second grade.

This leads us to the third rule about test scores:

3. *Do not rely on one score to predict school progress; the more test scores you have for a student, the more reliable the assessment.*

Had we relied on that one score in second grade, we would have been very wrong about Max's ability. Twelve years (!) of testing showed a consistent pattern of superior ability.

How Much Do Scores Vary and Why?

If your child were to take the same difficult test over and over again, the score your child received would vary to some extent. For example, a teacher could give the same test twice, as is often done with the weekly spelling test. The first time the child missed 5 out of the 20 words. The second time all the words were spelled correctly. Why? A number of explanations are possible, such as your child:

Practiced on two tests, so performance improved
Studied at home
Paid closer attention the second time
Happened to see a neighbor's paper the second time (and the neighbor was an excellent speller!)
Had been absent from school prior to the first test
The first test was only a practice test, and the child viewed the second test as more important and tried harder

As another example, let us say that at the end of grades 3, 6, and 8 a child was given a group test of intelligence. Again the three scores varied. This time there is little chance that practice would help the child score better because the tests were taken two to three years apart and the child would not remember. The child's IQ scores on the three tests might be 115, 110, and 108. Does this mean that the child was "smarter" on the first test? No. Each test has some room for variation. The publishers of tests must report typical variation on each test (called the *standard error*) and try to eliminate such sources of variation as poorly worded questions. When a test taken over and over results in widely different scores, the *reliability* of that test must be questioned. Reliability is the consistency with which a test measures what it intends to measure. If it is very consistent, it is very reliable.

Other factors can cause scores to vary, such as the attention paid by the child during the test; the child's comprehension of the test directions; the amount of guessing; and the health of the child on the day of testing. The teacher, aide, specialist, or psychologist must be prepared to identify any of these sources of variation when they are influencing the way a child functions, and then question the scores that result.

Wise is the teacher who, when reporting test results to parents, can say, "Something must have gone wrong when James took this test. The scores just do not fit with what James has done in the past. When I looked at the answer sheet, he was marking answers in the wrong column on the answer sheet on the reading comprehension test." Teachers need to review the children's actual answer sheets to pick up this type of error. Unfortunately many answer sheets go directly to a computer for processing so that the classroom teachers cannot review each child's answer sheet. But the alert teacher will question test scores that are out of line, and plan for a second testing where possible. Parents should *ask* for explanation of test scores that seem inconsistent with their child's previous performance. If in doubt, *ask* for a second testing.

What Does a Score Mean About Performance?

The scope of what a child knows can never be expressed in a single score. Only a small part of a child's many learning and life experiences can be tested at any one time. The repertoire of what your child knows, then, is much greater than the score he or she receives. However, a score can have a good deal of meaning if used in the correct way. For example, test scores gain meaning when they are used in relationship to the child's age, grade, and school curriculum. It would be meaningless to know a child's score on a mathematics test that measured understanding of new math if the child had not received new math instruction!

Each time a child is tested a sample is taken of what that child knows in a particular subject area or how well a child can perform a given skill.

We could not judge a baseball batter's skill based on only one trip up to bat. Neither can we judge a child's knowledge by one test score. The more scores we have, the better the measure we have of a child's performance.

Many tests are given to children as they progress through school. Some of these tests are developed by the classroom teacher and are given on a weekly basis and are called "teacher-made tests."

Teacher-made Classroom Tests

Most tests used in classrooms are developed by teachers to find out how much pupils have learned in the subject matter area they teach. As an important part of the ongoing classroom routine, teachers will test the progress of their pupils in mastering the subjects covered.

Most children encounter two kinds of teacher-made tests, (a) those assessing the child's mastery of specific individual learning objectives, (criterion-referenced) and (b) those assessing the child's performance as compared to the class (norm-referenced). The types of scores that result from both types of tests will be described next.

The first kind of testing is often referred to as *criterion-referenced* testing which asks: "How well does the child perform in relation to learning goals specified in terms of concrete behaviors?" A criterion-referenced test is used when a teacher is interested in looking at a child's performance in terms of whether or not the child has mastered specific learning behaviors, stated as behavioral objectives. The *criterion* is the child's mastery of the learning objective. The test results report the child's mastery only in terms of these behavioral (learning) objectives—"Jerry met the objective of adding with carrying two-place numbers with 90 percent accuracy." The child's progress through a series of specific learning objectives is monitored in this way through tests assessing mastery of each objective (sometimes called a mastery test) which assist the teacher in (1) matching instruction to pupil progress and (2) developing educational prescriptions to and for the child's pace and learning needs. Many school systems are finding it useful to report to parents their children's day-to-day progress in terms of mastery of objectives rather than by other kinds of scores.

The second kind of assessment, referred to as *norm-referenced* assessment, compares the child's performance to the performance of the class (norm). In the classroom this kind of test is graded on a curve that results in a grade score of A, B, C . . . or the percent correct (85 percent, 73 percent) which is later averaged with other test scores in order to assign the child a grade. This is the kind of assessment most parents experienced in school when they were pupils. The *criterion* here is the average performance of the group. The child's performance is compared to this average and receives a grade of A or B if above it, a grade of D or F if below it.

Both types of tests are useful in helping teachers and parents understand children. Yet there are important goals that are not easily assessed by tests. "Respecting the rights of others," "imagination," and "cooperation" are among important goals that a teacher cannot test easily. The teacher needs to observe systematically these characteristics after having determined beforehand what behaviors go into cooperation, imagination, and respecting the rights of others. This is not an easy task.

A *criterion-referenced test* is one in which the questions and scores that result relate performance to specific learning objectives. These tests are sometimes called *mastery tests* because they focus on the child's mastery of objectives. No emphasis is placed on comparing the child's performance or score with that of other children in the group.

In contrast, a *norm-referenced test* is one in which a child's score is compared with the average score of the group taking the test. This type of test helps teachers and parents understand the performance and progress of their child in relationship to other children of the same age or grade.

To summarize:

It is *very* important for parents to become informed about their child's achievement test scores and reports. Why? Because these scores will be used by the school staff to evaluate your child's progress; to place your child in certain classes or sections; to guide your child into major decisions about high school course options. These scores are as important to your child's school career as job evaluations and performance reviews are to the parents' careers. Pay attention to these scores! Learn to read them correctly! Ask for explanations! And keep complete records of all test scores.

CHAPTER 3

What Is an Intelligence Test? What Does an IQ Score Mean?

We can recognize a happy child as one who laughs a lot, who plays enthusiastically, and who talks animatedly about what is going on. We might agree that a project in a science fair reflects imagination. The child who is able to learn to read quickly and to calculate division problems readily is usually viewed as bright or intelligent. What do we mean when we say someone is "intelligent"? What does an intelligence test measure?

From early in our history to the present time, many abstract definitions of intelligence have been offered. While to date there is no one agreed upon definition, there is general agreement among psychologists, educators, and others as to behaviors that could be considered "intelligent." For example, if you were to be asked: How do you know that someone is intelligent? You might come up with behaviors such as "learns quickly," "has a good memory," and "can use past experiences," among others. Intelligence tests (frequently referred to as IQ tests) measure some of these behaviors.

Intelligence tests were developed in the early 1900s by Henri Binet and Theodore Simon to avoid judgments based on impression and prejudice. Before this, teachers had made decisions about which pupils were to be removed from the crowded schools. These decisions were thought to be subjective and often political. Under the direction of the French Commission of Education, it was the task of Binet and Simon to develop methods that were objective and to foster more adequate educational planning for below normal children. The results of the Binet test and of other intelligence tests have been used for their intended purpose, that of educational planning. Sometimes, however, their results have been misused to discriminate against the poor and minority groups, causing some people to question the value of these tests. If we were to throw these tests out, what alternatives would we have? We might find ourselves back in France in the 1900s, with pupil decisions made on the basis of subjective judgment open to bias, prejudice, and political influence.

"IQ" refers to "intelligence quotient." The introduction of this type of score dates back to Terman, who translated and revised the Binet tests for use in the U.S. Binet conceived of his first test of intelligence as a series of levels, each level being a "mental age." A child of 8, for example, could score a mental age of 10 years on Binet's test. Dividing a child's mental age in months (10 years = 120 months) by a child's chronological age in months (8 years = 8 × 12 = 96 months) (and multiplying by 100 to eliminate the decimal) produced an "intelligence quotient" first used on the Binet test. The formula became:

$$\frac{\text{Mental Age (MA)}}{\text{Chronological Age (CA)}} \times 100 = \text{IQ}$$

In this example, we have 120/96 = 1.25 × 100 = 125 IQ. The basic idea was that a child's mental growth, divided by its actual age, would give an IQ that reflected how more or less mentally developed a child's mind was, compared to the child's actual age. Today the IQ is no longer computed as MA divided by CA. Because IQ is a popular term, it has been retained. It is now derived from the normal distribution of score on tests so the average is 100, and the standard deviation is 15 or 16.

When used carefully and properly along with other information about the child, intelligence tests can provide helpful information to parents and teachers in making important educational decisions. Most special educational programs for the gifted and those for the handicapped require the use of intelligence tests along with other information for admission to such programs.

In the section that follows, we will describe the two basic types of intelligence tests that children are likely to encounter in school, *group* intelligence tests and *individual* intelligence tests, each of which have their own place in predicting school learning and aiding educational planning.

Group Tests of Intelligence

Group tests of intelligence are given in many schools every two to three years during a child's school history in order to predict school achievement. Although these tests may be used as early as the kindergarten level, they generally are not used before the second grade since children need to become familiar with the format of the kinds of tasks included. The directions are presented orally by the teacher to children in the class group, then each child responds to the picture or written choices from a group of choices. With younger children reading is not necessary, but as children progress through the grades, reading becomes more and more necessary to answer the questions. Therefore, group intelligence tests need to be used *very* cautiously in assessing the intelligence of children with reading problems. Group tests take from 30 minutes to an hour to administer.

Some commonly used group tests of intelligence include:

GROUP TESTS OF INTELLIGENCE

Test's Name	Abbreviation	Age Level	Type of Score Parent Might Receive
Cognitive Abilities Test (Formerly Lorge-Thorndike)	CAT	K–12	Verbal IQ or percentile rank Quantitative IQ or percentile rank Nonverbal IQ or percentile rank Overall IQ, percentile rank or stanine
Henmon-Nelson Tests	Henmon-Nelson	K–12	Overall IQ, percentile rank or stanine
Kuhlmann-Anderson Intelligence Tests	KA	K–12	Overall IQ or percentile rank
Otis-Lennon Mental Ability Test	Otis-Lennon	K/5–12	Overall IQ or percentile rank or stanine
Primary Mental Abilities Test	PMA	K–12	Mental Age (MA), overall IQ or percentile ranks
The Short Form Test of Academic Aptitude (Formerly California Test of Mental Maturity)	SFTAA	1–12	Language, nonlanguage and overall IQ score; percentile ranks, MA or stanine
Cooperative School and College Abilities Tests	SCAT	4–12	Verbal, quantitative, and total scores in percentiles or stanine

When used correctly, group tests of intelligence provide useful information about school ability levels, and help identify children in need of further assessment. A group IQ is a good step in estimating the appropriate level of achievement that can be expected for your child.

Individual Tests of Intelligence

As the name implies, these tests are administered individually to the child by a trained examiner, usually a psychologist. No reading is required on the part of the child, which is an important advantage if the child has a reading problem. The directions are presented orally by the examiner who can observe whether or not the child can understand the directions. The tests generally take 90 minutes to administer, and another 30 minutes to score. The most common individual tests of intelligence are:

INDIVIDUAL TESTS OF INTELLIGENCE

Test's Name	Abbreviation	Age Level	Type of Score Parent Might Receive
Stanford-Binet Intelligence Scale	S-B: Binet (called the Binet, pronounced "Bee-nay")	2–adult	Mental Age (MA) based on the number of items answered correctly IQ or percentile based on the child's chronological age and number of items answered correctly
Wechsler Preschool and Primary Scale of Intelligence	WPPSI (called "Wipsy")	4–6½	
Wechsler Intelligence Scale for Children Revised	WISC-R (pronounced "WISK-R")	6–16	Verbal IQ or percentile Performance IQ or percentile Full scale or percentile IQ which provides an overall estimate of ability
Wechsler Adult Intelligence Scale—Revised	WAIS-R (pronounced "Wace")	16–adult	
McCarthy Scales of Children's Abilities	MSCA (called the McCarthy)	2½–8½	General Cognitive Index (GCI) or percentile Mental Age Scale Indices (scores on various subparts of the test)

On each of these tests, the child's performance is compared with the average performance of children of the same age. The tests are made up of tasks of increasing difficulty. Many kinds of questions are asked that require the child to respond in different ways—by pointing, manipulating materials, and by speaking.

Individual tests are not given to all children because they are very expensive in terms of professional time. They are used when questions arise about a child's intelligence level and rate of school learning. They are required in many states as part of special education planning.

A small number of *brief* tests of intelligence are administered to some children individually for the purposes of *screening*, that is, identifying children who might benefit from more in-depth assessment of intelligence. For example, it is helpful to find out whether the child experiencing extreme difficulty in learning how to read is of average intelligence. If the answer is yes, this information helps the teacher make more effective remedial plans. If the answer is no, more in-depth intelligence testing may be warranted.

Some tests that the parents might encounter that fall within this group include:

SCREENING MEASURES OF INTELLIGENCE

Test's Name	Abbreviation	Age Level	What the Test Does; Type of Score Parent Might Receive
Columbia Mental Maturity Scale	CMMS	3–6 to 9–11 years	A test which does not require the child to make a verbal response and in which no reading is necessary. It assesses one area of reasoning ability by asking the child to point out which drawing in a group does not belong. For example, the child might need to point to a lamp as not belonging with a cup, plate, and fork. Scores include age deviation scores, percentile ranks, stanines, and maturity index (which is similar to MA)
Peabody Picture Vocabulary Test	PPVT	age 2½–18	Assesses only *one* aspect of intelligence, receptive vocabulary, which is the child's ability to identify one of four pictures that match the word spoken by the examiner. Some assessors view the PPVT as a screening measure of verbal intelligence. Scores reported can be IQ or receptive vocabulary scores, MA, and percentile ranks, *depending on the year of revision of the test.*
Pictorial Test of Intelligence	PTI	age 3–8	Used to screen the child's level of ability without requiring the child to respond verbally. The child needs only to indicate pictures that are the answer. Scores reported can be IQ, MA, or percentile ranks.
Ravens Coloured Progressive Matrices	CPM	age 5½–11	A test of the ability to use analogical reasoning to solve nonverbal problems. Scores reported are total correct and percentile.
Slossen Intelligence Test	SIT	age 4–18+	A brief screening instrument adapted from the Stanford-Binet. Most questions require the child to answer verbally. Scores reported can be IQ, MA, or percentile ranks.

What Is Normal Intelligence? What Is an Average IQ?

Children develop at different rates and have different abilities. These individual differences are with us for life as we engage in different jobs, hobbies, and ways of spending our free time. We also have different abilities to solve problems, to be long distance runners, to concentrate, and to be concert pianists. We are all different, yet there are average performances in all these areas. In school, there is also an average performance on tests. A test norm helps describe this performance.

A test norm is related to the "normal curve," sometimes called a "bell-shaped curve" because it is shaped somewhat like a bell. A "normal curve" is what happens if we pile up all the scores according to how each child scored. If we tested the IQs of all 5-year-old children in this country, they would receive different scores, but many children would score near the average. If we found the arithmetic average (referred to in statistics as the *mean*) of the IQs of all these 5-year-old children, we would be at the exact *center* of the normal curve. Many children would not test at the exact same score as the average, but would test a little higher or lower.

Look at the normal curve in figure 1. You can see how most children's scores pile up in the middle around the average. Fewer children score low, fewer score high. On a normal curve, the majority (68 percent) of scores fall between two points, between minus 1 and plus 1 *standard deviations*, from the average (or mean) of the curve. (A standard deviation

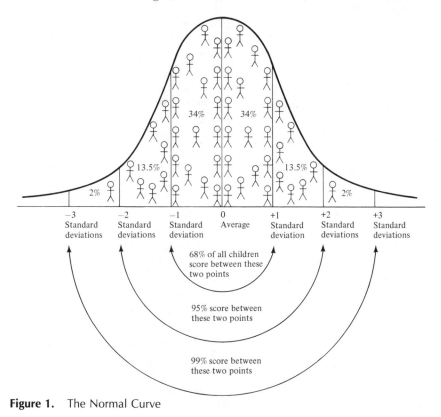

Figure 1. The Normal Curve

is a statistical expression of how scores vary—how spread out they are. A mean, or average, tells us how alike they are—how close together.) In figure 1, you can see that the biggest part of the bell curve is contained between minus two standard deviations and plus two standard deviations, and that this total is 95 percent of all the scores.

The normal curve is just a visual way to express what we all know, which is that many human characteristics are distributed normally, that is, on a normal curve. Most people are average in height, in weight, in intelligence, in eyesight, in ability to throw a ball, and in muscle strength. A few people are at the end of the curve for they are very tall, or very heavy, or very bright, or possess keen eyesight. A few are at the other end of the curve and they would be the very short, or the very thin, or have poor eyesight, or be slow to learn. Most of us fall somewhere in the middle.

Yet any one of us will vary from characteristic to characteristic. We may be in the middle of the normal curve on reading, above two standard deviations in mathematics, throwing a ball, music or riding a bicycle; but below two standard deviations in swimming, tennis, carpentry, art appreciation, or mechanical ability. None of us is average in everything. We will be average in one area, above in another, and below in another.

A very few people are extraordinarily talented. If we had a normal curve for musical talent, Mozart and Bach would be way above three standard deviations—way out at the very tip of the curve, into that rarely inhabited tip of the curve that we would reserve for genius.

Norms tell us where the *average* child scores on a test. If you look at figure 1 again notice that most children (68 percent) will score between plus and minus one standard deviation, which means that *most* children will score between 85 and 115 IQ on the most widely used individual intelligence tests. These scores are in the average range of IQs. Scores above 115 IQ to 130 IQ are considered above average; above 130 IQ is the superior level. Below average IQs are 85–70; under 70 is considered limited.

Stories you have heard about children scoring 200 on an IQ test are just plain nonsense! The top score on the Binet is 169, and the Wechsler about 150. Occasionally a child is very advanced at an early age, compared to his other contemporaries, and will score very high on the Binet—over 140, let us say. That happens at the preschool level occasionally with girls who are very verbal. But at an older age, that initial advantage may disappear. The other little girls (and boys) have developed verbally. Now our potential genius, Jeannie, scores 125 on the WISC. "What happened?" her parents agonize. "Did we fail our child?" No, parents, you did not. Your little Jeannie was a very mature four-year-old, compared to other four-year-olds. But at age ten, the others have caught up to Jeannie. A bright girl, who matured verbally ahead of the others, she now scores 125 which makes her above average. Lots of children show spurts at an early age. If the spurt is in verbal skills they will look very bright on IQ tests at that age. But *don't* label Jeannie a genius. Hold off! She's a "spurter," not a prodigy—wait to see her scores at eight or ten to avoid giving her an unrealistic view of herself.

What Are Age Norms?

Age norms tells us the average age of children getting the same number of questions right on a test. For example, let's say a test is given to many children of different ages with scores possible from 75 to 120. Age norms allow us to know the average score on that test made by children as they increase in age, usually reported on a month-by-month basis.

AGE SCORES FOR HYPOTHETICAL TEST

Age in Years and Months	Average Score on Our Hypothetical Test
Years/Months	
5 01	78
5 02	81
5 03	83
5 04	84
5 05	87
5 06	89
5 07	90
5 08	92
5 09	93
5 10	95
5 11	97
6 00	100
6 01	103
6 02	105
6 03	108
.	.
.	.

By looking at our example, we can see that the average child of 5 years and 6 months received a score of 89. It is then possible to find out a child's age score, no matter what the child's actual age is by comparing his or her score on the test with the age norms.

Many of the scores reported by tests that measure a child's development over time are actually age norms. Some other examples of scores that the parent might come across that are age norms are:

Mental Age (MA)—An MA of 100 corresponds to the average number of items on a test of ability correctly answered at each chronological age level. For example, on the Stanford-Binet, a mental age of 100 means that a child scored at the exact average (got the same number of items correct) as the average child of the same age (in years and months).

Educational Age (EA) or Learning Age (LA)—The EA or LA of the *average* child receiving each score on a test.

Social Age (SA)—The social age, usually expressed in years and months is the age equivalent to each score. "Social" here refers generally to tests that assess self-help skills (able to go to toilet unassisted, put on shoes, etc.), or to the child's skill/ability to interact with others (can play with another child, play games independently, respond to teacher questions, etc.).

Sometimes these scores are further translated into *quotients* by comparing the child's age score with his or her actual chronological age. For example a "learning quotient" would be determined by dividing the child's learning age by his or her chronological age and then multiplying the result by 100 (to get rid of decimals). The average quotient in all areas is usually 100.

Age norms are interpreted in much the same way as grade norms. The parent and teacher are usually interested in finding out whether the child is performing at a level that is equal to his or her chronological age, is at a level above or below it, and by how much. If, for example, a child of 6 years of age scores in the area of self-help skills like the typical child of 4 years of age, this would be an area the teacher and parent would want to work on with the child. If, however, this same child scored at a level typical of an older child, there would be no need for concern.

What Do Intelligence Scores Mean?

On all tests of intelligence the average score of all persons taking these tests is 100. Intelligence quotients that fall between 115 and 85 are in the "average range of intelligence." The higher an individual scores above 110, the more likely is the possibility that person will succeed with the kinds of tasks that are presented in school. Likewise, the lower one scores on an intelligence test, the greater the difficulty that person is likely to encounter with school learning. Some children are very handicapped and need special classes to help them cope with the demands of everyday living. Other children are very gifted and need special classes to help develop their special abilities. An intelligence test, however, does not tell the whole story. The child's motivation to learn, interest in the world, freedom from malnutrition and disease are all important points to consider when interpreting an IQ score. We have all heard stories of late bloomers or persons whose abilities went unrecognized during their early years in school.

For most children, however, an IQ score provides one estimate of ability and helps to set levels of expectations for the child so that we neither set levels that are too low and without challenge, nor too high that are overdemanding. Intelligence test scores help us understand when a learning disability is interfering with a child's learning. Other information must be taken into account as well.

In order to dispel some of the mystique that surrounds intelligence test scores, table 2 provides information about scores, the labels attached to them, and the percentage of people attaining these scores. Please note the *percentiles*.

Table 2
INTELLIGENCE TEST SCORES AND THEIR MEANING
(The Wechsler and Binet Tests)

	Approximate % of Children Receiving Score	Wechsler IQ	Binet IQ	Percentile
Superior	1.5–2%	130+	140–169[1]	97–99
Above Average	7–11%	120–129	120–139[1]	89–97
	14.5–16%	110–119	110–119	73–89
Average	46–50%	90–109	90–109	26–72[2]
Below Average	14.5–16%	80–89	80–89	10–25
	5.5–7%	70–79	70–79	3–10
Limited	2–3%	69 and below	30–69	1–3

[1]Note that Binet scores are much higher than Wechsler scores to fall in the same percentile range.
[2]The child with an IQ score of 100 would be performing at the 50th percentile.

If teachers or schools are reluctant to tell you your child's IQ score, you can estimate it by using the above chart. Please note that the 26th to the 72nd percentile is encompassed by the *average* range of IQ!

Many teachers and schools are reluctant to tell parents a child's IQ score, based on two widespread, but mistaken beliefs. First, there is a widespread belief, which is in error, that an IQ score equals intelligence. Intelligence is much more than one test can measure. The second mistaken belief is that an IQ score in some way is fixed or unchanging. IQ scores often do change as the child matures and has different experiences, and it may change up or it may change down.

In table 2, it is particularly important to look at the percentile translations of scores. It immediately becomes apparent, for example, that a score of 130 on a Wechsler tests falls at the same percentile level as an IQ score on the Binet of 140. The children are scoring at exactly the same level, one is not smarter than the other. This example illustrates why a score alone does not tell the whole story. Ask for your child's IQ in *percentiles*!

Questions Frequently Asked About Intelligence Tests and Their Answers

What Kind of Questions Will My Child Be Asked?

Questions about general information such as: "How many months are in a year?"

Questions that ask the child to reason, such as: "In what way are a dog and a cat the same?"

Questions that ask a child to think about pictures, such as: "What is missing in this picture?"

Questions that tap the child's vocabulary and ability to comprehend, such as: "What does 'happy' mean?" or "Put the cup under the table."

Questions that ask children to use numbers such as: "If John had 5 pennies and Mary had 2 pennies, how many would they have altogether?"

Questions that involve memory, such as: "I want you to say what I say—The cat is sleeping."

Questions that involve copying, such as: "Make one just like this one."

Questions that involve sequencing and puzzles such as: "Here are some pictures that I want you to put together so they tell a story."

Questions such as: "What number comes next?"

What Is an Intelligence Test?

An intelligence test is one measure of the child's ability to handle school learning tasks. Some people consider it a measure of how quickly children are likely to learn in school.

How Do Most Children Perform on an Intelligence Test?

The exact average IQ score of all children across the country is 100 and the average range includes IQ scores from 85 to 115.

Should the School Report the IQ Score?

Yes, we feel strongly the school should, with an appropriate explanation of what it means, how it can vary, and how the score can change if different tests are used.

Should Children Be Placed in Special Programs Based on IQ?

Never on an IQ score alone. You as parents have every right to insist that

IQ scores be accompanied by achievement tests, health information, and classroom observations.

What Decisions Are Based on the Results of Intelligence Tests?

The most important use of intelligence test results is program planning for the child. Used along with other information about the child, teachers and parents can be helped to set appropriate goals for children.

What Is the Difference Between the Verbal IQ Score and the Performance IQ Score?

The verbal IQ score is based on the child's ability to handle thinking questions that require a spoken response. Test questions that assess verbal abilities include those that ask the child to define words and to comprehend situations.

The performance IQ score is also based on the child's ability to analyze and comprehend situations, but the items presented *do not* require the child to make a verbal response. Instead the child might be asked to point to what is missing in a picture or to put together puzzles.

Do IQ Scores Change?

Yes! As children grow older tests measure different things. IQ scores can go up and can go down.

What Abbreviations Appear on Test Results? What Do They Mean?

Some common abbreviations you may find when the results of intelligence tests are reported include the following (also see the Glossary for the meaning of these terms):

IQ—Intelligence Quotient. This is a translation of the child's overall score on test of intelligence. This score is arrived at by comparing the number of questions answered by your child to the average number of questions answered by children of the same age in the group on whom the test was standardized.

CA—Chronological Age = the child's age in years and months on the day the test was taken.

VIQ—Verbal Intelligence Quotient. The score on that part of the test made up of questions that require a verbal answer.

PIQ—Performance Intelligence Quotient. The score on that part of the test made up of questions that do not require a verbal response.

FSIQ—Full Scale Intelligent Quotient. Another way of referring to the child's *overall* IQ score.

GCI—General Cognitive Index. The overall score obtained on the McCarthy Scales.

LQ—Learning Quotient. The overall score on any test that relates the number of questions answered by the child to the scores of the average child of the same age taking the test.

Refer to the Glossary for a definition of any term or abbreviation that is unfamiliar to you, so you can be fully informed.

CHAPTER 4

The Most Frequently Used Achievement Tests and What They Measure

Children take many standardized achievement tests throughout their school career, usually on a yearly basis. As the name implies, an achievement test is one that assesses the child's school achievement in such subjects as reading, mathematics, language, social studies, science, and sometimes in the area of study skills. These tests are generally administered at three points during the school year, depending on questions the school system hopes to answer. They are administered (1) during October or November to measure what was learned the previous year and to plan instruction; (2) midway through the school year in January or February, and these results are given to this year's teacher, as a measure of the school's effectiveness and to plan instruction; (3) during the spring (April–June) which puts emphasis on this year's teacher and to effectiveness of instructional programs.

Most achievement tests children take are group tests, that is, given to classrooms of children at one time. Some measure children's skill in one area such as reading, while others are actually batteries of tests to assess children's mastery of a number of areas of instruction. Whereas some achievement tests provide an overall impression of a child's achievement in a given learning area (sometimes called "achievement survey tests"), others provide more specific and detailed information and are called "diagnostic achievement tests." A summary follows in alphabetical order of some of the popular achievement tests children might encounter. The specific test used by school systems depends on the match of that test to the school's curriculum, and to the background and needs of the children involved. The general content areas covered by each of the popular achievement tests will be indicated, but remember that the content covered and level of the test depends upon the age and grade of the child.

FREQUENTLY USED ACHIEVEMENT TESTS

Test	Grade Levels Covered	Content Areas Covered	Type of Scores Parent Might Receive
California Achievement Test (CAT) (CTB/McGraw-Hill)	1.5–12	Reading: vocabulary, comprehension Mathematics: computation, concepts, problems Language: mechanics, usage and structure, spelling	Percentile ranks Stanines Grade equivalent scores By subtest area and for the total test
Comprehensive Tests of Basic Skills (CTBS) (CTB/McGraw-Hill)	2.5–12	Reading: vocabulary, comprehension Language: mechanics, expression, spelling Arithmetic: computation, concepts, applications Study skills: using references and graphic materials	Percentile ranks Stanines Grade equivalent scores By subtest area and for the total test
Educational Records Bureau Comprehensive Testing Program (ERB) Achievement Test	2–12	Reading: vocabulary, comprehension (listening and word analysis grades 2–3)	Percentile ranks Stanines By subtest and for the total test

Test	Grades	Subtests	Scores	
Educational Records Bureau Comprehensive Testing Program (ERB) Achievement Test		Mathematics: concepts / computation		
		Writing skills: spelling / capitalization and punctuation		
		English expression		
Aptitude Test		Verbal / Quantitative / Total		
Iowa Tests of Basic Skills (ITBS) (Hieronymus, Lindquist, and Hoover)	1–8	Vocabulary	Grade equivalent scores	By subtest area and for the total test
		Reading: word analysis skills / comprehension	Age equivalent scores	
		Language: spelling / capitalization / punctuation and usage	Percentile ranks / Stanines	
		Mathematics: concepts / computation		
		Work-study skills: map reading / reading graphs and tables / knowledge and use of references		

FREQUENTLY USED ACHIEVEMENT TESTS (Continued)

Test	Grade Levels Covered	Content Areas Covered	Type of Scores Parent Might Receive
Iowa Tests of Educational Development (ITED)	9–12	Reading: comprehension vocabulary total Language arts: usage spelling total Mathematics Composite Social studies background Science background Use of sources	Standard scores Growth scale values Percentile ranks Stanines	By area and clusters of areas
Metropolitan Achievement Test (MAT) (Prescott, Balow, Hogan, and Farr)	K.1–12	Word knowledge (vocabulary) Word analysis Reading (comprehension) Language (punctuation capitalization, and usage) Spelling Mathematics: computation concepts problem solving Science (facts and concepts) Social studies (facts and concepts; using maps and charts)	Percentile ranks Stanines Grade equivalent scores	By subtest and for total test

Test	Grade/Age range	Subtests/Content	Score types	Norms
Cooperative School and College Ability Tests (SCAT), Series II	4–14	Verbal Quantitative	Converted scores Percentile ranks Percentile bands Stanines	By subtest and for total test
SRA Achievement Series (Naslund, Thorpe, and Lefever)	K–12	Reading: Visual discrimination Reading: Auditory discrimination Reading: Letters and sounds Reading: Listening comprehension Reading: Vocabulary Reading: Comprehension Mathematics: Concepts Mathematics: Computation Mathematics: Problem solving Language arts: Mechanics Language arts: Usage Language arts: Spelling Reference materials Social studies Science	Grade equivalents Percentile ranks Percentile bands Stanines Normal curve equivalents	
Sequential Tests of Educational Progress (STEP) Series II (Educational Testing Service)	4–14	Depending on grade level: Reading Mechanics of writing English expression Mathematics computation Mathematics basic concepts Science Social studies	Percentile ranks Percentile bands Stanines	
Stanford Achievement Tests (SAT)* (Madden, Gardner, Rudman, Karlsen, and Merwin)	1.5–9.5	Vocabulary Reading comprehension Work-study skills Mathematics: concepts computation applications	Stanines Grade equivalent scores Percentiles Age scores	By subtest and for total test

FREQUENTLY USED ACHIEVEMENT TESTS (Continued)

Test	Grade Levels Covered	Content Areas Covered	Type of Scores Parent Might Receive
Stanford Early School Achievement Test	K–1	Environment Mathematics Letters and sounds Aural comprehension	Raw scores Percentiles Stanines
Stanford Test of Academic Skills (TASK)	8–12	Spelling Language Social science Science Listening comprehension Reading English and spelling Mathematics	Percentile ranks Stanines
Tests of Academic Progress (TAP)	9–12	Social studies Composition Science Reading Mathematics Literature	Percentiles Standard scores

*Not to be confused with the SATs taken in high school, Scholastic Aptitude Test (SAT).

It is important for teachers and parents to keep in mind that the scores from one test to another can be very different in meaning and need to be interpreted with caution.

Sometimes the teacher or other educational specialist would like to have achievement information about an individual child and may administer an individual achievement test. Some individual achievement tests such as the *Wide Range Achievement Test* (WRAT) provide a very quick sample of the achievement areas assessed; others provide more comprehensive diagnostic assessment of a particular learning area such as the *Key Math Diagnostic Arithmetic Test.* Some of the individually administered achievement tests are listed below.

INDIVIDUALLY ADMINISTERED ACHIEVEMENT TESTS

Test	Grade Level	Content Covered	Type of Scores
Peabody Individual Achievement Test* (PIAT) (Dunn and Markwardt)	K–12	Mathematics Reading recognition Reading comprehension Spelling General information	Age equivalent scores Grade equivalent scores Percentile ranks
Wide Range Achievement Test (WRAT) (Jastak and Jastak)	K–adult	Reading (word recognition) Spelling Arithmetic	Grade equivalent scores Percentile ranks Stanines
Woodcock Johnson Psycho-educational Battery* (Woodcock and Johnson)	Age 3– adult	Cognitive ability Achievement Interest level	Age equivalent scores Grade equivalent scores Percentile ranks

*Diagnostic instrument.

The achievement tests described up to this point serve three purposes: (1) to measure skill development, (2) to compare the level of a child's performance to other children of the same age and grade, and (3) to identify pupils who might need comprehensive *diagnostic* assessment. The names of some of the diagnostic tests that cover subject matter in detail are presented in the next section. These tests can be administered either individually or to a group. They help to pinpoint specific areas of a pupil's strength or weakness. Some of these focus on only one subject area, and others cover more than one subject area.

Diagnostic Tests of Achievement

Most of the tests we have referred to thus far assess the child's overall achievement in basic subject matter areas. Other tests, such as the Key Math Diagnostic Arithmetic Test are diagnostic in that they help pinpoint specific areas of pupil strengths or difficulty, and attempt to get at the reasons for these difficulties. By discovering the kinds of errors children make, the teacher is helped to focus on specific learning areas in which the child needs practice and sometimes, based on trial learning activities, on alternative procedures that might work when teaching the child. Diagnostic tests are important since they can lead to the development of remedial programs. The basic skill areas of reading, arithmetic, spelling, and language are essential to the child's learning and future success in school. Therefore most diagnostic tests focus on these areas. Most of these tests are administered individually to the child so that the teacher or specialist administering the test can observe the child's approach to completing the tasks as well as his or her answers.

DIAGNOSTIC LEARNING TESTS

Test	Grade Level	Content Covered	Type of Scores
READING			
Diagnostic Reading Scales, Revised Edition (Spache)	1–8	Word recognition Reading passages Oral and silent reading Skills assessed	Grade equivalents
Gates-MacGinitie Reading Tests (Gates and MacGinitie)	K–12	Vocabulary Comprehension	Grade equivalents Percentile ranks Standard scores
Stanford Diagnostic Reading Test (Karlsen, Madden, and Gardner)	1.6–13	Word analysis Comprehension Reading rate, scanning and skimming Auditory discrimination Blending Rate of reading	Norm-referenced scores Percentile ranks Grade equivalents Stanines Content-referenced scores Progress indicators
Woodcock Reading Mastery Tests (Woodcock)	K–12	Skill development in the areas of: letter identification word identification word attack skills word comprehension passage comprehension	Percentile ranks Grade scores Age scores
ARITHMETIC			
Basic Skills in Arithmetic (Wrinkle, Sanders and Kendel)	6–12	Assesses proficiency in basic processes of addition, subtraction, multiplication, and division	Percentile ranks
Key Math Diagnostic Arithmetic Test (Connolly, Nachtman, and Prittchett)	Pre-School–6	Assess proficiency in three areas: content, operations, and applications	Grade equivalents Performance area scores Subtest scores

Stanford Diagnostic Mathematics Test (SDMT) (Beatty, Madden, Gardner, and Karlsen)	1.5–High School	Assesses mastery in three areas: number system and numeration, computation, and applications	Scaled scores Grade equivalents Percentile ranks Stanines

SPELLING

Test of Written Spelling (Larsen and Hammill)	1–8	Assesses spelling to apply both rule-governed and non-rule-governed words that are dictated	Spelling age Spelling quotient Grade equivalents
Spellmaster (Cohen and Abrams)	K–adult	Spelling of regular words, irregular words, and homonyms Diagnostic assessment of pupils analysis and spelling ability requiring them to know how to apply phonetic and structural elements.	Individual progress level (ungraded)

Other Tests of Achievement

Achievement tests are available in other academic areas as well. Again, their purpose is to monitor pupil progress in specific subject matter areas. The results are also used to help make placement decisions as well as to plan instruction. For example, the *Pimsleur Foreign Language Proficiency Tests* assess listening, speaking, reading, and writing proficiency in French, Spanish, and German, and are used by schools to help decide if and when a pupil should study a foreign language.

The results of achievement tests, whether given to groups of pupils or individually administered, serve to:

1. Monitor skill development in academic subjects
2. Compare the pupil's performance to that of other pupils of the same age and grade
3. Identify pupils needing more comprehensive assessment
4. Help pinpoint areas of strength or problem areas
5. Help schools evaluate whether a particular instructional program has been successful
6. Help determine whether pupils should repeat a grade, or skip a grade
7. Determine whether pupils have achieved the minimal competencies for graduation

"Competency" tests are achievement tests. Many states have developed their own tests to assess competency. The grades at which competency tests are administered differ by state and are summarized in the helpful publication *Parents Can Understand Testing* by Henry S. Dyer (see Appendix G).

CHAPTER 5

Questions Parents Should Ask at School and How to Ask Them

One day soon you will be faced with an important school conference on your child's progress in school. Following are some of the questions that you should be prepared to ask about your child's testing performance. In each case we will try to suggest ways to phrase your questions for the teachers and administrators with whom you will be dealing, and also some examples of ways *not* to ask questions.

Question 1: What Is My Child's IQ?

Whatever else you may think about IQ scores, they are still the best single predictor of how a child will do in formal schooling. An IQ score will not predict how well your child will do in ballet, on the ski slopes, at tennis, or photographing wild animals in East Africa. What it *does* predict is how fast your child will learn traditional school material in comparison to other children of your child's age. Therefore it is crucial that you be familiar with your child's IQ test scores.

Knowing your child's IQ is the best way you have of setting a reasonable expectation for your child's progress in school. You want to set reasonable expectations, not unreasonable ones. So the very first thing you want to find out is his or her most recent IQ score. It is obvious that if you walk in and say "I want to know my child's most recent IQ score!" you are very likely to put up the backs of the school personnel. They will think you are abrupt, that you are trying to pretend you know a lot about IQs, and that you are going to use test information in a way that will not be helpful to your child. So let's not start off that way.

Let the school people start the conference telling you *why* they want to have it. This may be a routine conference to check on your child's progress or it may be a conference called to deal with a special matter. Let the school people set the stage and tell you how they view your child's progress. After a few minutes, you will need to find an opening to talk about test scores. It might come about like this:

SCHOOL PERSONNEL: . . . and the reason we wanted to talk to you at this time, Mr. and Mrs. Johnson, is our concern that Jean is not keeping up in her Spanish and we wonder if she has been doing her work at home and if she has really been doing the best she could in it.

PARENT: That is one of our concerns also, and one thing that has been on our mind is whether or not we are setting the right kinds of expectations for our Jean. We don't want to expect too much from her, but we don't, on the other hand, want to set too low an expectation. It would be very helpful to us if you could share some of her test scores with us so we would know what to expect of her in comparison to the other children. For example, one thing we have been concerned about is her IQ score.

This is one way to do it, and a way that shows you as a parent concerned with setting a fair level of expectation. Most school people will react very favorably to that kind of approach.

In asking for an IQ score, you should be aware that the test records of your child are available for you to see, in fact are covered by the Buckley Amendment discussed in Chapter 7. If school officials tell you that you cannot see your child's permanent record or your child's test scores, they are simply in error, and you need to point out to them that you have the right to see these under the Buckley Amendment. Under *no* circumstances should you permit yourself to be refused this right. It is better to do this in a polite and agreeable way. If you meet with serious resistance, then you may have to indicate that it is your legal right to see these records, and if the school refuses, that the school will have a suit on its hands.

As the teacher (or counselor or principal) begins to share your child's permanent record and test results with you, you want to make a very important move. Pull out the paper and pen you brought for this purpose on which you can make notes. This is important because it alerts the school personnel that you plan to make a record yourself of what you are about to hear, so they will take pains to see that you get the right information written down. Here is a sample conversation about an IQ score, and a girl named *Jean.*

COUNSELOR: Let me see. I think the most recent IQ score we have on Jean is from last year when we—let me see—the record here says her IQ score was 103.[1]

---

[1]We would not encourage parents to rely on only one IQ score, as is done in this example, but to ask instead for a second test, if at all possible.

PARENT: Let me make a record of that because I can't trust my memory on these things. You said 103?
COUNSELOR: Yes, 103.
PARENT: Could you tell me the name of that test, please?
COUNSELOR: That was on the Otis-Lennon.
PARENT: The Otis-Lennon? What kind of test is that?
COUNSELOR: That's what we call a group test.
PARENT: What is a group test, please?
COUNSELOR: That means the test was given to all the children at the same time in the group.
PARENT: Is there another kind of test besides the group test?
COUNSELOR: Yes, there is an individual test in which the child takes the test alone with a psychologist.
PARENT: I see. Which test is a better one for parents to base their expectations on, do you think?
COUNSELOR: I would think that the individual test is probably a more reliable indicator.
PARENT: I see. So what we have is a 103 on the Otis-Lennon, which is a group test, which Jean did last year when she was in ninth grade. Do we have a record of an individual test score for her at some point?
COUNSELOR: No, we don't do that routinely. That sort of test is only given to children about whom we have some very special concerns.
PARENT: I see. Jean hasn't been that kind of concern then, so we'll have to go by this group test, is that right?
COUNSELOR: Yes, I think you can consider that a pretty good estimate of her ability.

At this point the parent has learned two very important things, one of which is their child's actual IQ score on a particular test. The parent has also learned that Jeannie's learning has not been of sufficient concern to her teachers to have had an individual IQ test requested. But what the parent now needs to know is what the 103 really means.

PARENT: This IQ score of 103—how does Jeannie compare to the other children in this school in IQ?
COUNSELOR: That's a good question. We think our average IQ here is between 105 and 110.
PARENT: I seem to remember something about the normal curve. Isn't it true that most of the youngsters will be clustered around the average and very few at the top and at the bottom?
COUNSELOR: Yes, that's true.
PARENT: Then how does 103 stack up against your average? What percentage of the youngsters, let's say, would be at 103 as compared to 105 or 110?
COUNSELOR: I would estimate that this would put Jeannie at the 30th percentile in our school population.

PARENT: The 30th percentile? That means that she can learn faster than 30% of them, but will be slower than 70%, is that what you mean?

COUNSELOR: Yes, that's a good way of putting it.

PARENT: Well, that puts a different light on things as far as we're concerned. 103 sounds all right when we talk about an average of 100, but really with the children concentrated as they are around the school average of 105–110, that really means that our Jean is competing at a disadvantage in this school, isn't she?

COUNSELOR: Yes, you might say that. To some extent she is learning a little bit more slowly than the other children.

PARENT: The 30th percentile means she is below 70 percent of this school, does it not?

COUNSELOR: Yes, for *this* school, which is above average. But she is average for all students across the country.

PARENT: Well, at this point we're taking it step by step. What should an IQ score tell us as parents?

COUNSELOR: It's a good test of how fast your child learns school material in comparison to other children.

PARENT: I thought that was what you had implied. And I think then we should take this quite seriously, shouldn't we?

COUNSELOR: Yes, I think you should.

PARENT: Let me repeat it, so we're sure we get it straight. What this test score means, if we assume it is an accurate one, is that our Jean is not learning as fast as 70% of the children here, but is learning faster than 30%. If there were 100 children in the school and if they were ranked from smartest to slowest, she would be the 70th person in the line starting from the smartest.

COUNSELOR: Yes, that's quite correct, and I think you have to take this into account in evaluating what Jean's progress should be here in the school.

What the parent should be concerned about now is whether they want to rely on the estimate of their child's IQ based on the group test. A group test is a very good test in many ways because it duplicates the conditions under which most children learn in school, which is in groups. However, many people feel that it is only a half hour sample of a child's work and that it relies heavily on reading ability. An individual intelligence test, which takes an hour and a half, is administered according to some very strict standards by a trained psychologist and may provide a better estimate of ability. What the counselor might have been wiser to suggest at this point is that an individual test be given to see how Jean performs compared to her IQ score of 103 from last year. The parents may choose to have the testing done in the school if there is time, or they may choose to have it done outside. In any event it would be a wise thing for the parents to discuss if they want a good estimate of what they should be expecting from Jean.

Question 2: What Are the Earlier IQ Scores?

If there had been earlier IQ test scores, the parents should have asked for them, and recorded the date on which the test was given, the name of the test, and the actual score. Let's assume that Jean had had other group IQ tests, which is probably the case for most children. In the ninth grade, we know she had the Otis-Lennon and received 103. Let us assume in the sixth grade she had another group test and received an IQ of 110. In the first grade she was given still a different group IQ test and got a 112. What are the parents to think? Are they to assume that Jean has been getting dumber over the years because she went from 112 to 110 to 103? What the parents should be thinking is that test scores vary somewhat over time, and test scores vary by the test that is given. So it is to be expected that there will be a change from year to year. Their best piece of information is that these three scores are not that different over such a long period of time. Considering that they are derived from different tests, there is a fairly consistent pattern here. It is not as though Jean tested at 135 one year and 95 the next, which would be an extraordinary difference. What they can tell from these test scores is that Jeannie has tested within roughly the normal range since she started school, and with an IQ now of 103, that puts her slightly above the exact average in the country which is 100. But in this particular school, the counselor tells us, they have a somewhat select population and the children are a little above the average.

Question 3: What Are My Child's Achievement Test Results?

Now that Jean's parents have the information that Jean is probably of average intelligence but appears somewhat less fast at her learning than the other children in her school, they have some basis in which to interpret the achievement test results. So the parents proceed this way.

PARENT: I think that has been very helpful. I wonder if we could now discuss some of her achievement test results so we can get a picture of how she is progressing in school.

COUNSELOR: Surely. I'll be glad to share that with you. Her most recent achievement test results were done this fall in tenth grade. In her reading abilities she was at the 40th percentile and in her mathematical abilities she was at the 51st percentile.

PARENT: When you say she is at this or that percentile, what are you comparing her to?

COUNSELOR: I'm sorry. I should have explained that. We are comparing Jean's performance to those children on whom the test was standardized, and that represents a statewide sample of all children in school in the tenth grade.

PARENT: And what is the name of that test, please?

COUNSELOR: That is the statewide test given to all tenth graders in the state.

PARENT: I see, and that suggests that Jeannie is doing just what we would expect, from her IQ score, isn't she, on her verbal and on mathematical abilities?

COUNSELOR: Yes, I think that's fair to say. In the first instance we were comparing her to the children in this school, which is a fairly selective public school. On the statewide test we are comparing her to all the children in the state who take the test, so there are two different comparisons being made.

PARENT: I see. What you are saying to us, I guess, is that although Jean may not be quite as smart as the average youngster in this school, she does pretty well in comparison to all children in the state who are in the tenth grade.

COUNSELOR: That's exactly right.

PARENT: What does that mean for the future?

COUNSELOR: It means that Jeannie is about average compared to all the tenth graders in the state on these abilities which are supposed to be the best predictors for later school work. Now we have to remember that all the tenth graders in the state do not go on to college, about 50 percent of them go on to some sort of post-secondary education, such as a community college or a technical college or 4-year college, but those that do go on are self-selective, which is to say they tend to be those students who do better in school.

PARENT: What does that mean for Jean? Does it mean she will be able to go to some type of college or not?

COUNSELOR: It means she will be able to go on to a college, but we will have to be very careful in what we help her select, because we do not want to put her in a place that's much too competitive for her.

PARENT: I see. Can you help us with these choices?

COUNSELOR: Yes, I'll be very glad to do so.

What the parents learn here is that 103 in high school A may not be an advantage, in fact it may be a disadvantage, but in comparison to all the other children in the state, 103 is close to the middle. The question of what a child should be compared to is always arising. It reminds us of a favorite story about Mark Twain. One day he was asked by a friend, "How is your wife?" to which Mark Twain replied "Compared to what?" If we took a perfectly healthy average youngster and placed him or her in a very competitive high school, of which there are a number in the country (very selective and attracting very special youngsters who have particular abilities), that perfectly healthy, normal child would look very slow indeed in that population, and would have a great deal of trouble keeping up. The same thing is true of college placement. A youngster with an IQ score of 103 may do well in a certain kind of college, and find that they can keep up with the work. Let us say that Jean decides to go to a community college, for example, and she may find that she can handle it, especially if she has good work habits, but it would be grossly unfair to expect Jeannie to enter and compete in a college where the average IQ may be 120 to 130. That is like putting a young horse of average ability into the Kentucky Derby and expecting it to do well.

Let us take a different look at achievement test results at a younger age level to see how they might affect a parent's evaluation. This time we have parents coming in about their son, Carl, who is in fourth grade. They have gone through the same sort of information seeking as the parents did with their daughter Jean, and Carl's parents have learned that Carl's IQ score is 108 when tested this fall on an individual intelligence test. They then asked to be told about his achievement test results.

SCHOOL PSYCHOLOGIST: We have some very interesting test results on Carl. When I saw the achievement test results I wondered if we shouldn't go ahead with an individual achievement test, which I would like to discuss with you today, but let me share these with you first. Now Carl was in the fourth grade in December when these were given, and as you know, achievement test results like these are reported in grade equivalents. It means that if this was an average school, children in it should be doing work at the fourth year grade, and at the fourth month of the school year, because we count it from the middle of September to October to November and December so that would be the fourth grade, fourth month when these tests were given on December 17. If everything were perfectly normal, the test results would come back at about 4 years, 4 months in December of the fourth grade. However, this school is not exactly at the average, it is a little bit above. We find really that our children are 4 to 6 months ahead of this kind of progress. Most children in his class are doing somewhere between 4 years, 7 months and 5 years on these tests. Now Carl's class averaged on this reading test a grade score of 5.1, which is quite good, meaning that they were about 7 months ahead of the national average on this particular reading test. But Carl scored 3.4, meaning that he is reading at the level of third grade, fourth month, instead of fourth grade, fourth month, which puts him a full year behind an average class, and almost a year and a half behind this particular class in his reading ability.

PARENT: Well, that's serious, isn't it? I had no idea that he was that far behind.

SCHOOL PSYCHOLOGIST: I don't think it is serious in the sense of a permanent problem. But I do think it is fair to say that he is 1–1½ years behind in his reading, depending upon whether you are comparing him to the whole country or to this particular grade in school. I prefer to compare him to the school he's in, because that's where he's competing with his classmates, and here he is a year and a half behind.

PARENT: I don't understand why that is. We just found out that he has an about average IQ for this school, I think you said 108, and yet he is 1½ years behind in reading. Why is that?

SCHOOL PSYCHOLOGIST: I don't know why at present, because I don't have enough information. One reason I wanted to see you is that I want to do more testing with Carl to see if we can pinpoint where the trouble is coming from. His IQ on the individual test would suggest that he is capable of doing the work, but the reading test certainly suggests that he is way behind.

PARENT: Do you have any other test scores that would help us understand this?

SCHOOL PSYCHOLOGIST: Yes, we have his math score which is 4.5, which would put him just about equal to the rest of the class. They were about 4.5 also. But his spelling is down. That's about 3.2, and the class is around 4.5 on the spelling. So, he's okay in math, but down in reading and in spelling.

PARENT: You should see his handwriting! Do you think that has anything to do with it? It's the worst I've ever seen. I don't know how he can read it.

SCHOOL PSYCHOLOGIST: Yes, I do think it does have something to do with it. Many boys we see are like this—it seems to happen much more often in boys than girls—they have a combination of trouble with reading, writing, and spelling. That is a very common pattern.

PARENT: Do you think this writing and reading and spelling pattern is all some sort of block?

SCHOOL PSYCHOLOGIST: I don't think I would call it a block. I think I don't have enough information yet to tell you what might be part of the difficulty, but I would like to suggest that we go ahead and do another individual intelligence test on Carl to make sure we have a sound estimate of his ability. Then I'd like to do some analysis of his reading skills and of spelling and see if we can figure out where the trouble is and make some plans to remedy it.

In the example above, Carl is a child who not only was of normal intelligence, average for that particular school, but who showed a real deficit in the language arts area of reading-writing-spelling, although his mathematics score was fine. These scores suggest that we are dealing with a learning problem in one area, not one across the board. If all the scores were down—in reading as well as mathematics and social studies—it would suggest a very different problem, such as a generalized learning problem, or a generalized lack of motivation, and possibly a real problem in all forms of learning. Where we see an adequate IQ score and a deficit in one area, it is more likely to be something related to that one area itself and the way the child is learning in it, and is more likely to be helped with appropriate instruction.

Question 4: How Does the School Interpret These Test Results?

One thing that the parents want to achieve in a conference, once they have recorded the test results of their child, is to ask the school to respond to these test scores and to tell them the school's interpretation. In the instance of Carl, just cited above, the school psychologist made a sensible recommendation which was to do more diagnostic testing to see if the trouble could be pinpointed. It is important to get the school's acknowledgement that the scores lead to some sort of course of *action* that needs to be taken. The school needs to respond to data that are contradictory, or inconsistent, or that suggest something is out of order between the child and what the child is learning.

Question 5: How Does the School Plan to Act?

Somewhere toward the end of the conference, and after reviewing the test data, the parents should try to elicit from the school personnel what their plan of action is going to be. It may be that the next step is to gather more information and that can be a very appropriate next step, but eventually some plan of action has to be formulated. If Jean is not learning well in Spanish, several plans come to mind easily. One is that maybe Jean should not be in Spanish. Not every person in this world is endowed with the talent and interest to pursue a foreign language when they are 15 years of age. There are many other ways to learn a language than in high school or in grade school, for that matter, so that one is not giving up a priceless and lifetime chance to learn a foreign language. With children who are somewhat behind others in their rate of learning, as in Jean's case, one obvious step is to lighten the child's load so that he or she doesn't have as much to try to learn in the same period of time as the faster kids do. In the case of Carl who appears to have some type of reading problem, once the reading problem has been identified, one expects the school to recommend a course of action, which might mean extra instruction, or a different kind of instruction, and/or help into the summer, and/or specific kinds of practice at home. The school might suggest many other plans, but the parents can expect at least one or two plans to be suggested, and furthermore, to be followed up to see if they are effective. Here is one way this could be handled.

COUNSELOR: So you see we really don't know why she is having so much trouble in Spanish.
PARENT: It seems to me that we ought to be talking about some course of action. I think Jean is struggling with her Spanish. We can see she is trying very hard at it, but I just think it is very hard for her to do and I am wondering what you think in view of these test results.

COUNSELOR: Well, I suppose it is a bit of a struggle for her, but I would hate to see her lose Spanish.

PARENT: I don't know that she has to lose Spanish forever, but I wonder whether she has to have it right now.

COUNSELOR: Well, I suppose that is a possibility, but I hate to take her out of there, when I think she is learning something.

PARENT: Yes, but I don't like to see her overburdened either. What do you generally recommend in a case like this?

COUNSELOR: Well, it depends on the circumstances. Sometimes the youngster may not really be trying as hard as he or she might.

PARENT: I don't think that is the case here with Jean. We all see a very hard-working young lady here and your own test scores suggest that she is doing quite well, picking it up as well as she is doing.

COUNSELOR: Yes, I would have to say that she is and everyone certainly likes her.

PARENT: Well, what options do we have besides dropping her from Spanish? What else would you suggest?

COUNSELOR: Well, we could leave her in Spanish and get her some extra help until the end of the year.

PARENT: But isn't that just increasing her work load rather than decreasing it?

COUNSELOR: How do you mean?

PARENT: I mean we are talking about a youngster who is having trouble keeping up with the race, as it is, and we're asking her to carry not only Spanish, but extra instruction in Spanish and that means increasing her academic load. I would think that what we should do is to reduce her academic load, don't you think?

COUNSELOR: Well, it is up to you and Jean, really. That's not something that we would like to recommend without the parent's full approval.

PARENT: What is the alternative?

COUNSELOR: Again, I would say extra instruction and maybe even summer school if she doesn't pass Spanish.

PARENT: I just don't see ruining Jean's summer because of Spanish. I don't care if she learns Spanish while she is in high school. She can learn it some other time if it's important to her, and there are other ways to learn than so many times a week, don't you think?

COUNSELOR: Yes, I suppose that's true.

In the example above the parents took a much more aggressive role than many parents might be willing to take. However, the parents were justified, for the *last* thing one wants to do to a youngster who is not learning as fast as other children, is to *increase* their work load. Jean, you will recall, appeared to be in the 30th percentile of her high school, which is to say she is below the average in her speed of learning. The first step for the counselor to recommend is an individual intelligence test if it confirms the group IQ of 103. Then Jean will take longer to learn the same material than the other children in her school, in fact, more than 70 percent of the other children. It would be very unusual for it to be a good solution to simply add more work to that youngster's load. The world will not end if she comes out of Spanish, or in fact, any other subject, unless it is absolutely essential for graduation.

The school's reaction to test data in terms of the plans they come up with, is a key to the flexibility of the school in adapting to individual needs. Schools in general are not really run for individual needs. They are run for what is best for most people and for the school's organization. So parents must shoulder the responsibility of informing school personnel constantly about individual needs of their own children and try to get the school to make reasonable adaptations to those needs. We are of the strong opinion that *some* children should not take gym, and *some* children should not take Spanish, and *some* children should not take geometry, and *some* children should not take algebra, and *some* children should not take shop, and *some* children should not take art, or music, and so on. In short, there are instances in which almost any subject is an abnormally difficult subject for some children, due to their natural abilities, or some experience they have had, or the way their heads work.

We take the attitude there really *are* individual differences in learning! The job of the parent is to insist that these be recognized on behalf of their own child, without asking the school to stand on its head. We do not subscribe, on the other hand, to the idea that schools should be expected to provide lessons in Greek for the one child in thousands who has a spontaneous interest in Greek. But we do see the school's need to be flexible within what they have to offer.

Question 6: How Do I Evaluate Competence in a Remedial Plan?

One thing that parents need to be alert to is competence of the professional with whom they are dealing. Not all teachers, or counselors, or specialists, or school psychologists, or principals are equally competent. It is a very delicate matter to assess the competence of the professional with whom you are dealing, but it is important to try to do so. Let us assume that the recommendation is made that Carl get some tutoring in reading. Parents need to use some judgment in picking outside tutoring help for their children. Not all tutors are equal, by any means. Here is one way that a parent could question professional competence.

SCHOOL PSYCHOLOGIST: . . . and I would like to recommend to you two or three names of reading tutors that we have found to be very helpful to children here. I would suggest that you take down the names of Mrs. Schneider, Mr. Allsop, and Ms. Straight. I will give you their phones and addresses before you go.

PARENT: It would be very helpful to us if you could tell us the kinds of things we should look for in choosing a tutor. I mean, how do parents know when they are getting a good tutor as compared to one who is not so good?

SCHOOL PSYCHOLOGIST: That's a good question and a hard one to answer. Here at school we go by the results pretty much. We learn over a period of time what children seem to be helped more by one tutor than another, and then we make the recommendations that that person be used. I think one thing you can do is call the parents of some of the children that these people have worked with. I'll give you the names of some parents before you go.

PARENT: That will be very helpful. How would I know when the tutor really was doing a good job?

SCHOOL PSYCHOLOGIST: That's not an easy question to answer. One thing I would look for is whether or not Carl likes to work with the tutor you pick. But you have to understand that it's not likely he'll be over-joyed at spending more time in reading when reading is already diffi-cult for him. I wouldn't want the tutor to spend all of the time playing games with him just to get him to like it, because there has to be some work involved, but a good tutor generally will find pleasant ways to get children to practice skills. The next thing I would look for is whether or not Carl is picking up on his skills. I'd make a point of having him read with you once a week, anyhow, and of looking at his writing or his spelling, depending on what the tutor is working on, to see if you notice any improvement.

PARENT: Well, what about testing? Isn't this a good place to use tests to see how he is improving?

SCHOOL PSYCHOLOGIST: Yes, I think that is a good suggestion, as long as we don't expect to see him jump way up in a matter of a few weeks. Reading improvement does not come overnight by any means, and I would think you would want to wait at least three months before testing him to see if he's coming up.

PARENT: Well, how do I tell about the tutor's training? What should I look for in their training that would help me select a person?

SCHOOL PSYCHOLOGIST: That's also not easy. Generally a tutor has a master's in their subject area, such as a master's in reading if they are doing some remedial reading, and generally they have had experience as classroom teachers. But it's hard to say whether lots of years of experience is better or worse than fewer years.

PARENT: What do I ask them? Do I ask them where they have been trained?

SCHOOL PSYCHOLOGIST: Yes, I certainly think you can ask them for a vita (pronounced "vee-tah"), or ask them over the phone about their train-ing. I would simply say that you are ignorant in this area and would like to become informed about tutoring.

PARENT: What else can I do?

SCHOOL PSYCHOLOGIST: I think what I would do if it were my own youngster is to ask each tutor to lay out a plan of what he or she plans to do, to sit down with me and show me the plan for the next three months, so I would have some sense of what the tutor was trying to accomplish. That would give me some idea of whether or not the effects of the extra instruction were going to be very useful. I would then check to see whether or not the plan is being followed. I'd ask to see Carl's books and the exercises he was doing, and I'd ask the tutor to check with me once every two weeks and let me know how he was doing.

The suggestions that the school psychologist made above were good ones. It is very hard to pick a tutor by training only because there is nothing to distinguish a good one from a bad one by degree level beyond a master's level. The recommendations made by the school personnel is one good source, although you want to be careful they are not recommending teachers on their staff just in order for them to pick up extra income. Tutoring is a way for teachers to supplement their salaries. It is an appropriate thing for them to do, but you want to be assured that it is not the major reason for a recommendation. Calling the parents who have hired the tutors is a good move because it gives a sense of how tutors work, how well they get along with children, and whether or not they have shown some results as other parents see it. It certainly behooves a parent to spend the money to sit down with the tutor for an hour to have the tutor explain *precisely* what he or she is going to do, the materials he or she is going to employ, the games or exercises that he or she is going to use.

There is no reason in this world why a parent should not understand exactly what the tutor is attempting to accomplish, because there is nothing that mysterious about remedial help in any subject matter that would keep a parent from understanding a tutoring plan. As part of the plan, one would hope that the tutor would find enjoyable ways to employ drills. There is no way around a certain kind of drilling, such as building up sight words in the vocabulary. But good tutors and good computer programs are ingenious at devising clever games and variations to relieve the boredom of this. No normal child is going to want to sit down to memorize sight words, flash card after flash card, for an hour. So a good tutor and a good computer program break up the time with small units, varying the drill with different kinds of games, different kinds of practice, and preferably, using some rewards.

Question 7: What About Follow-up?

Before the conference has ended, the parents should make notes on the same piece of paper on what the follow-up plans will be. If they are told their child should have additional testing, then the parents should ask the school personnel when the testing is to be completed. It is often true that schools cannot say exactly when something is going to be done, but they can give the parents an outside date by saying, "It will be done no later than . . ." in order that the information be useful to the school. The parent should get that date nailed down and write it on that piece of paper. Whatever other steps are going to occur should have a time related to them. For example, if one was to consider dropping a child from Spanish, it is important to know whether it is to be done this week, next Monday, or two weeks from now, because the parents want to know and they want their child to know. If tutoring is to be started, the parents need to know the date when it will begin and how the tutoring will be coordinated with the teacher.

After the conference is finished, it is a good idea for the parent to write a letter to the school staff thanking them for the conference, pointing out several things that will be very helpful, and putting in writing the agreement on the follow-up steps and when they are to take place. It is a nice way to say thank you to the school staff, and also it is a nice way to make a contract about future steps so that they are not left up in the air.

If there are any rules for handling this type of conference, they are:

1. Don't be afraid to ask anything you want to know about your child.
2. Ask it as positively as you can.
3. Ask because you want to learn. School personnel love to teach.
4. Write it down.

CHAPTER 6

Aptitude, Interest, and Personality Tests: What They Can and Cannot Do

Beginning in the junior high school years, aptitude, interest, and personality tests may be given to your child as part of vocational and educational planning carried out by the school.

Aptitude Tests

An aptitude test assesses aptitude, i.e., a child's latent ability in such skills as mechanics, art, clerical procedures, foreign languages, and so on. Aptitude test results help make instructional choices by predicting a match between the child's abilities and the alternative areas of specialization available in the high school curriculum. Such tests help teachers and counselors in planning the young person's school curriculum and in discussing future vocational plans.

Parents should be alert to the importance of the decisions made by the beginning of the eighth or ninth grade about their child's high school course. Most high schools offer at least these three tracks, sometimes located in separate schools:

Academic track: Student will go on to a 2-year or 4-year college
Vocational track: Student will take training in auto trades, mechanics, electrical work, carpentry, etc., and after high school will seek a job in these trades or go on to a technical school.
Secretarial-Commercial: Student takes training in office skills (typing, stenography, computers) and after high school will seek an office job or go on to further technical training.

In rural areas, students can elect "vo-ag," a vocational agriculture specialization which is an increasingly popular choice for students. Vo-ag can lead to a 4-year college degree, or to a 2-year associate degree in some aspect of agriculture, or to a job after high school.

What is imperative is for parents to recognize that the track your child selects in the beginning of ninth grade is usually a *final* choice, one that will affect not just the high school years, but your child's immediate post-high school opportunities for further education. If your child is mechanically inclined, he can elect a trade school track, but if he has academic ability sufficient to take him through a college of engineering, he should consider the academic track.

Not all children should go to college, by any means. The trades are now having a revival in attracting young men and women who prefer the life of a carpenter or gardener to that of commuting business executive.

The ninth-grade decision, which is made at the end of the *eighth* grade, is very influential in immediate post-high school education, so it should be taken *very* seriously and carefully. Even though you may be advised that your child can shift from one track to another later on, and that the track decision at the end of the eighth grade is a reversible one, the practical implication is that the decision is rarely changeable. Why? Because a student who elects trade school or the commercial track spends so much time on these courses that were he or she to switch to the academic track by January, or even November, this student would be so far behind that the job of catching up to the academic track students would be overwhelming for most students.

So this is an important reason why parents should take the results of aptitude tests seriously, particularly if they will be used to elect one high school track rather than another.

One of the most widely used tests of aptitude is called the *Differential Aptitude Test* (DAT), usually given in eighth grade for high school planning. The DAT is actually a battery of tests to help guide the young person in making educational and vocational choices. The following areas are assessed by the DAT: verbal reasoning, numerical ability, abstract reasoning, clerical speed and accuracy, mechanical reasoning, space relations, spelling, and language usage.

The results of these tests are likely to be reported to the parent, teacher, and student in terms of percentiles, stanines, and percentile bands. Pay special attention to the *combined* scores of verbal reasoning (VR) and numerical ability (NA) as they are used as predictors of success in the academic track and for college success. Ask your guidance counselor to tell you what level of combined scores indicate a strong aptitude for college, both two and four year.

Other aptitude tests assess the child's ability in specialized areas. Some examples of these are listed here.

TESTS OF SPECIAL APTITUDES

Subject Area	Grade	Test and What It Measures
Music	4–12	*Seashore Test of Musical Talent* assesses memory of tones in children.
Foreign languages	7–adult	*Pimsleur Language Proficiency Tests* and *Modern Language Aptitude Test* assess the child's talent for learning foreign languages.
Algebra	H.S.	*Orleans Hanna Algebra Prognosis Test*
Clerical aptitudes	7–12	*Minnesota Clerical Aptitude Test* can be used to assess clerical aptitudes in children (also the DAT clerical subtest).
Mechanical aptitude	11–12	*Bennett Mechanical Comprehension Test* can be used to assess mechanical aptitude in students.

Interest Inventories

Since student interests and motivation play an important role in careers, interests are assessed through questionnaires and inventories. These are used along with the results of tests such as the DAT in planning for careers. While neither aptitude tests nor interest inventories can predict who will actually succeed in his or her career, the greater one's interest in one's work, the more likely one will stick with that work and be satisfied with it. Some tests that help measure student interests are listed here.

TESTS OF INTERESTS

Test	Grade	What It Measures
Strong Vocational Interest Blank (SVIB), or Strong-Campbell Interest Inventory (SCII)	H.S.	These inventories assess a student's interest in specific occupational areas, comparing them to the interests of persons already in these areas, persons in occupations such as farmer, artist, teacher, lawyer, forester, army officer, etc.
Kuder Vocational Preference Record (Kuder)	6–12	This inventory is used to assess general areas of interest, rather than specific occupational interests. The general areas included are outdoor, mechanical, computational, scientific, persuasive, artistic, literary, musical, social service, and clerical.
Gordon Occupational Checklist	8–12	This checklist helps assess general occupational interests in five broad areas related to business, outdoors, arts and entertainment, technology, and services.
Minnesota Vocational Interest Inventory	H.S.	This inventory is used to help assess the interests of students who are *not* college bound, such as plumber, mechanic, baker, etc.

Attitude, Adjustment, and Personality Measures

One's personality includes attitudes, motivations, emotions, and reactions to experiences. It is these personality traits that are measured by attitude and personality tests. We would all probably agree that a child's motivation, likes and dislikes, attitudes, and emotional adjustment affect the way in which he or she learns in school. The depressed or very unhappy child will not be able to learn efficiently. Although learning and a child's adjustment cannot be separated clearly, most tests used in school focus on learning, since this is the major job of the school. When emotional or adjustment problems affect the child's learning, a trained person, usually a psychologist or guidance counselor, may be called upon to help understand and plan help for the child.

Attitude Tests

The attitudes children develop through their life experiences are likely to affect the way in which they react to other children and to the school situation. The pupil who has positive attitudes toward school is likely to achieve better than the pupil with poor attitudes toward school. Attitude tests include problem checklists, inventories, and self-concept tests which are likely to be used with younger children. These attitude tests are not tests in the usual sense of the term, for there are neither right nor wrong answers. Rather, these tests and inventories consist of a series of statements which pupils check as applying to themselves, or which teachers check as an accurate observation. These measures can help teachers and counselors identify areas that *might* be troublesome in health, study skills, peer relationships, home and family, work, and plans for the future. Some examples of these measures are included here.

TESTS OF ATTITUDES

Checklist	Grade	What It Measures
Behavior Problem Checklist (Quay and Peterson)	K–6	This checklist is used with children to help identify problems of social behavior or conduct that can interfere with school functioning.
Joseph Pre-School and Primary Self-Concept Screening Test (Joseph)	Pre-school–5	This screening test is used by teachers to identify at an early age those children who may be experiencing problems.
Mooney Problem Checklist (Mooney)	7–12	This checklist is used by pupils to help identify problems of concern to them at home and at school.
Piers-Harris Children's Self-Concept Scale (Piers and Harris)	3–above	This scale is used by children to get at feelings of satisfaction about themselves.
Walker Problem Behavior Identification Checklist (Walker)	4–6	This checklist is used by teachers to observe behaviors that might suggest problem areas to be watched more carefully.

Attitude tests, along with observation and talking with pupils, can help teachers become aware of the attitudes their pupils hold, which in turn can influence their teaching. Since attitudes tend to change, the results of attitude measures need to be used very carefully. Interpretation needs to be made by the trained counselor or psycholgist.

Personality Measures

Personality measures likely to be used in schools include personality inventories and projective tests. Again, there are no right or wrong answers on these measures. The responses pupils make are used to help identify individuals with possible problems who may need additional attention or help. "Self-assurance" and "socialization" are examples of traits assessed by such measures as the following.

PERSONALITY TESTS

Test	Grade	Purported to Measure
California Psychological Inventory (Gough)	7–above	Personality structure problems
Minnesota Counseling Inventory (Berdie and Layton)	H.S.	Personality structure problems

In contrast to other measures which ask pupils to check statements or to make choices among statements, another type of measure sometimes used in schools is the projective test. With projective tests the individual responds to ambiguous pictures or figures by making up stories or by telling what they see. For example, in the *Thematic Apperception Test* (TAT) the student is asked to tell stories about a series of pictures. An adaption of this test, the *Children's Apperception Test* (CAT) is sometimes used with young children. The *Rorschach* requires the individual to tell what they see in ambiguous figures which are actually inkblots. Many answers are possible and there are no right or wrong answers. Sometimes children are asked to draw pictures of persons and other objects such as a house or tree in order to gain some idea of their perception of the world in which they live. The assumption with each of these types of tests is that a child's responses will provide clues about how he or she feels about himself or herself and their world, providing the trained psychologist with some insights into their thinking and feeling.

Projective tests, however, are not used frequently in schools since they must be used by trained psychologists. There is also considerable disagreement among psychologists as to the worth of projective tests. For that reason they have not been covered in detail here. In schools it is more likely that classroom observation and interviews will help teachers, counselors, and psychologists gain an understanding of a student's difficulties.

CHAPTER 7

What a Parent Needs to Know About School Records

As a parent you will be very interested in the tests your child takes in school and in their results. By inquiring about your child's progress, recorded on your child's school record, you can help assure the proper use of these tests and records. You will also understand more about your child's ability. You can also become an active and informed partner with the school in educational planning for your child.

You may have been concerned about what actually goes into your child's school record (also called *cumulative record*). In 1975 the General Education Provisions Act (generally known as the Buckley Amendment)[1] legislated the right of parents across the nation to have access to their children's records. Students above 18 years of age or enrolled in college also were given the right to see their own educational records. However, the privacy of the information on educational records must be safeguarded. There are likely to be many interpretations of this law, as with most laws. Access to records may be facilitated in some school systems and hindered in others. Either way, parents have the right—and may insist upon it if necessary—to see their children's school record.

Parents *should know* the facts about their child's school progress, including their test scores. It is true that not all parents are equally familiar with test results. In our opinion, it is the responsibility of educators to make meaningful interpretations of school records to parents. If test scores are there to help educators make objective judgments about children, they are also there to help *parents* make objective judgments about their own son or daughter.

[1]*Federal Register*, vol. 30, no. 3, January 6, 1975.

What Do School Records Contain?

School records generally contain information about the child in a number of categories, such as:

Background Information About the Child's Family

Information is recorded which can help the school get in touch with the child's family in case of an emergency, as well as information that might be important when planning the child's school program. Typically the information is gathered when the child is first enrolled in a school, and includes:

Name of mother/father/guardian
Address
Telephone number
Work location and sometimes occupation of mother/father/guardian
Birthplace of mother/father and child
Other children in the family and their ages
Language spoken in the home and by the child

Information About the Child

Information is recorded about the child's health and language background relevant to planning the child's school program. Some schools maintain separate health records for children. In this section is usually recorded:

Sex of child
Date of birth
Whether or not the child speaks English—if not, what language is spoken
School changes along with the date of entrance into the new school
Days absent (which might indicate that the child has missed important instruction units)
Health information regarding vision, hearing, speech, previous illnesses, physical problems, medication taken

Yearly Record of the Child

In this section the academic record of the child is recorded year by year, as well as the child's attendance record. Again the information gathered in this section is used in the yearly planning of children's programs and includes:

Grades given by the child's teachers in each subject area. These may
be recorded by the year only, or by each marking period as well

Scores obtained by the child on standardized tests

Teacher comments at the end of each year, sometimes for each
marking period

Indication of the child's special interests, talents, and activities

Indication of interviews held with the child or with his or her parents

Grades or comments regarding conduct, self-help skills, and ability
to interact with others.

Examples of various sections of pupil record forms are shown below.
Some variation in format is likely to occur from one school system to
another; however, most pupil cumulative records are likely to contain
much of the information illustrated.

SAMPLE A: PUPIL CUMULATIVE RECORD
Background Information About the Child's Family, and
Information About the Child

Last name First Middle	Place of Birth	Sex Date of Birth M F — — — ☐ ☐ mo. day yr.	Date of Entrance Grade
Address	Tel. Number	Siblings	
Father's Name	Place of Birth	Place of Work Tel. Number	
Mother's Name	Place of Birth	Place of Work Tel. Number	
Name of Guardian	Address		Tel. Number
Language Used in Home Language Used by Child		Previous Schools Attended Dates	

Summary of Attendance							
	19__ 19__	19__ 19__	19__ 19__	19__ 19__	19__ 19__	19__ 19__	
Days Present							
Days Absent							
Times Late							

SAMPLE B: PUPIL CUMULATIVE RECORD
Yearly Record: Secondary School—Academic Record

	YEARLY SCHOLASTIC RECORD											
		Marks* Quarters							Marks* Quarters			
Year	Subjects	1	2	3	4	Credits	Year	Subjects	1	2	3	4	Credits
19__	English						19__	English					
to	History						to	History					
19__	Science ( )						19__	Science					
	Algebra I							Algebra II					
	French I							French III					
	Physical Ed.							Physical Ed.					
	English							English					
19__	History						19__	History					
to	Geometry						to						
19__	French II						19__						
	Physical Ed.												
	Elective**												

*Trimesters or whatever number of marking periods is used by the school.
**Electives may include such areas as shop, typing, art, cooking, psychology, anthropology, etc.

			ACHIEVEMENT TEST RECORD																		
Class	Date	Name of Test	Form Level ***				Subject Areas Covered														
			SS	0/0+	ST	SS	0/0+	ST	SS	0/0+	ST	SS	0/0+	ST	SS	0/0+	ST	SS	0/0+	ST
I																				
II																				
III																				
IV																				

***SS = Standard Score % + = percentile ST = Stanine These terms were explained in chapter 2.

SAMPLE C: PUPIL CUMULATIVE RECORD*
Yearly Record: Elementary School

YEARLY SCHOLASTIC RECORD										
Grade	Date of Graduation:									
Year and Term	19__ 19__	19__ 19__	19__ 19__	19__ 19__	19__ 19__	19__ 19__	19__ 19__	19__ 19__	19__ 19__	19__ 19__
Subjects										
Reading										
Spelling										
Penmanship										
Language										
Mathematics										
Social Studies (geog.)										
Science										
Art/Music										
Physical Ed.										
Sewing/Cooking**										
Industrial Arts (shop)**										

*Filled according to subjects and areas of emphasis.
**Generally apply to seventh and eighth grade.

SAMPLES OF RATINGS USED ON PUPIL CUMULATIVE RECORD:
ACADEMIC RECORD

RATING KEY

E—Excellent	S—Superior	S—Satisfactory
G—Good	A—Average	NI—Needs Improvement
F—Fair	U—Unsatisfactory	U—Unsatisfactory

90–100	A—Excellent
80–90	B—Good
70–80	C—Fair
Below 70	D—Poor
Below 60	F—Failure

Achievement Test Record

Grade (class)	Date	Name of Test	Form Level	Subject Area Covered																	
				RS *	GE **	%tile ***	RS	GE	%tile	RS	GE	%tile	RS	GE	%tile	RS	GE	%tile	RS	GE	%tile

*RS—Raw Score or Standard Score
**GE—Grade Equivalent or Age Equivalent
***%tile—Percentile

SAMPLE D: PUPIL CUMULATIVE RECORD
Yearly Record: Elementary and Secondary School—Intelligence Tests

Group and Individual Intelligence Tests

		Group									Individual					
Grade	Date	Name of Test	Form	V	NV	IQ	%tile	Grade	Date	Name of Test	Form	CA	MA	VIQ	PIQ	IQ	%tile

Key to abbreviations: V—Verbal; NV—Nonverbal; IQ—IQ score; %tile—Percentile; CA—Chronological Age; MA—Mental Age; VIQ—Verbal IQ; PIQ—Performance IQ; IQ—Overall IQ; %tile—Percentile.

SAMPLE E: PUPIL CUMULATIVE RECORD
Other Information Recorded

Special Interests and Talents	Year/Date

Activities, Clubs; Out-of-School Activities, Jobs	

Special Disabilities; Needs	

Social-Personal Behavior	
Responsibility Cooperation Self-control Participation	

Interviews	
Date Person & Interviewer Comment	Date Person Interviewed Comment

Comments/Consultations	

School records maintained by the school psychologist, social worker, or school physician are not always open to parent inspection on the assumption that such records require specialized training to understand. In some states such as New York, however, reports based on the individual psychological examination conducted in the public schools are also open to inspection by parents, and students above the age of 18. Since these records are often housed in a different place than the child's academic record, the parent will need to make a special arrangement to see these records, and to request that an appropriately trained person be present to provide explanations and answer questions that might arise. These records should be maintained in accordance with ethical standards

SAMPLE HEALTH RECORD

Last Name	First	Middle		Sex Male Female		Date of Birth Mo. Day Year			
Address						Tel. Number			
Immunizations Date:				Medications					
	Grade__ Date__	Grade__ Date__	Grade__ Date__	Grade__ Date__	Grade__ Date__	Grade__ Date__	Grade__ Date__	Grade__ Date__	Grade__ Date__	Grade__ Date__
Height										
Weight										
Vision										
Hearing										
Teeth										
Speech										
General										
Other										

of the respective professional organizations. Parents can have access to these professionals by requesting conferences with them.

Records maintained by schools are important for planning instruction, keeping track of pupil progress, for guidance and counseling for specialized training, college selection, or work choices, and the evaluation of instructional programs in schools. But records can be abused in at least four ways when parents do not have access to them.

As was pointed out in a report by the Russell Sage Foundation,[2] parents need to be aware of the following kinds of potential abuse:

[2]Goslin, D. *Guidelines for the Collection, Maintenance and Dissemination of Pupil Records* (New York: Russell Sage Foundation, 1970).

1. When outdated information is not updated or destroyed
2. When inaccurate information is not removed
3. When certain information is collected without parent consent, such as personality test data, or when information recorded for one purpose is used for another
4. When records are viewed by nonauthorized personnel

The parent can help prevent such abuses and assist the school to keep accurate and current by:

1. Informing the school of changes such as a change in a parent's telephone number, address, or telephone at the place of work in case of an emergency
2. Requesting changes in inaccurate information or in facts that have changed
3. Giving permission for appropriate persons to see records

Questions Relating to School Records

What are some questions a parent might want to raise with the school staff about his or her child's school record?

Is my child progressing as he or she should be? Is my child achieving at a level consistent with my child's ability?

How does my child compare with other children in his or her class in terms of ability and achievement?

Are there areas of particular academic strength or weakness in my child? To what extent is my child mastering the goals of the curriculum at this grade level?

Has there been a decline in performance in reading or mathematics or in another subject from one year to another?

How many days was my child absent during the school year which might have resulted in some important practice being missed? What specific areas were missed?

What test scores were recorded and what do they mean for my child?

Does the school have an idea of my child's interests and talents?

Does the school have a picture of my child's special needs?

Do teacher comments reveal a problem about which I am unaware?

Teacher Comments

Teacher comments are included on records to note important observations. Teacher comments can range from useful, objective information about the child, to subjective and sometimes inappropriate anecdotes. Some examples of useful information teacher comments can provide include important developmental milestones that have been reached. For the very young child, the ability to engage in group play or to hop and skip are important observations to be noted. As children progress through the grades, observations recorded by teachers can help identify special interests or potential problems to assist the succeeding year's teacher. Information such as "Vera seems to become particularly restless before lunch," "Lucy is a shy and quiet child who can be helped to participate through verbal praise," "Jerome's interest in sports has helped him tackle difficult reading material in that area," and "Matthew needs work in developing study skills" are all important observations about children that can be of help in furthering their education.

Sometimes infrequent behaviors are noted about a child such as "Judy tends to be a trouble maker" or "Pete is disruptive." When these are the only comments recorded, parents should inquire into the frequency of such behavior and about the events leading up to it. If these cannot be documented, such comments might better not be placed on records which follow a child from year to year.

While teacher comments can provide helpful information about children, it is important that the behaviors recorded are (1) typical of the child and (2) can be used productively in planning his or her school program.

Classroom Records

In addition to the child's cumulative record kept in the school office, the classroom teacher often maintains a folder for each pupil, which contains more detailed information about performance on each area of standardized achievement tests, along with work samples and important observations about the child. The information in this folder can be shared with parents during parent-teacher conferences.

Records for Research Purposes

It is both legitimate and necessary for the school to be engaged in ongoing research to understand more about how children learn, and to evaluate the effectiveness of teaching programs. Information on children's academic performance is often necessary to carry out such studies. It is important that information on pupil's performance be collected so as to keep the identity of all children anonymous. Most of such information concerning school performance does not constitute an invasion of privacy if the child is not going to be identified, so the parent's permission is not required. For example, data collected for purposes of understanding the effectiveness of certain reading programs might include the sex and age of children, grade, reading programs used, and reading achievement scores. The identity of each child would be anonymous and each child's privacy protected. In contrast, a study of home influences on children's school motivation would generally require the consent of parents for collection of data on individual pupils, so a consent form would have to be signed by the parent.

Reading a School Record Accurately

We will conclude this chapter with an example of a school record for one fourth-grade pupil, whom we will call Tony Martin. (In the school system Tony attends, a separate health record is maintained for pupils which will not be illustrated here.)

PUPIL CUMULATIVE RECORD
Background Information

Name *(Tony)* Anthony G. Martin	Place of Birth San Francisco Calif.	Date of Birth Sept. 28, 1971	Sex Ⓜ F

Address 2314 Main St. Any Town, U.S.A.	Telephone Number 723-4567

Mother's Name Mary	Business Address 237 First St.	Business Telephone 739-1234
Father's Name George	Business Address 15 River St.	Business Telephone 684-5678
Name of Guardian	Address	Telephone

School: *Central School, Anytown, N.Y.*   Date Entered *12/3/79* Grade *3*

Previous Schools: *Davis School, St. Claire, Texas*   Dates From: *2/4/77* To: *11/30/79*

Siblings: Maryann *(Twin)*	Date of Birth Sept. 28, 1971	Language Used in Home: English
George Jr.	June 15, 1969	Language Used by Child: English

Attendance Year	1977 1978	1978 1979	1979 1980	1980 1981	1981 1982	19__ 19__	19__ 19__	19__ 19__	19__ 19__
Days Absent			10	12	9				
Days Present			113	163	166				
Times Late			2	1	1				

From this part of the school record we know the following information which can help teachers to plan for Tony:

1. Tony and his family moved to this community and Central School in December of his third grade year. Prior to that he attended only one other school–Davis School, from 1977–1979.
2. Tony has a twin sister and one brother, two years older.
3. English is spoken in Tony's home.
4. Tony's attendance record is fairly good.

From the part of the school record shown on page 87 we know that Tony:

1. Performs at least at an average level in all areas.
2. His strengths lie in the areas of social studies and science, and he does well in physical education.
3. His areas of relative weakness lie in the areas of reading and penmanship, although some improvement has been indicated during the last school year. We might want to follow Tony's progress in this area and possibly check out his reading speed, since there was some decline in his mathematics grades, and we know that mathematics increasingly require the child to read and solve problems.
4. Tony does well in physical education and probably enjoys sports.

From the record of the group test of intelligence administered in third grade (shown on page 88) we know that Tony has above average intellectual abilities, with an IQ of 114. This information causes us to begin to question why he has been performing at the C or C– level in those areas that call upon reading.

SAMPLE PUPIL CUMULATIVE RECORD
Other Information Recorded

Special Interests and Talents	Year/Date
Plays the trumpet	*5/12/79*
Activities, Clubs; Out-of-School Activities, Jobs	
Cub Scouts	
Special Disabilities; Needs	

SAMPLE PUPIL CUMULATIVE RECORD (Continued)
Other Information Recorded

Social-Personal Behavior			
	6/79	6/80	6/81
Responsibility	+	+	+
Cooperation	+	+	+
Self-control	+	+	+
Participation	+	+	+

Interviews						
Date	Person & Interviewer	Comment	Date	Person Interviewed	Comments

Comments/Consultations	
Tony enjoys sports and is well respected by members of his class (5/80)	

From this component of the record we learn that Tony is a cooperative
and responsible member of his class who enjoys music and sports.

SAMPLE PUPIL CUMULATIVE RECORD

ACHIEVEMENT TEST RECORD											
Grade (Class)	Date	Name of Test	Form/ Level	Total Battery		Auditory		Reading		Mathematics	
				Stan.	%tile	Stan.	%tile	Stan.	%tile	Stan.	%tile
3	Mar. 3, 1980	Stanford Achievement	IIIa	5	56	6	66	5	42	7	84
4	Ap. 6, 1981	Stanford Achievement	Interm Ia	6	62	6	64	4	36	7	88
5	Ap. 13, 1982	Stanford Achievement	Interm IIa	6	66	7	88	4	34	6	76

On the Stanford Achievement Test, the following areas are tested:

Auditory—Includes subtests which assess vocabulary and listening
comprehension

Yearly Scholastic Record

Date of Graduation: _____

Grade										
Year and Term	19__ 19__	19__ 19__	19<u>29</u> 19<u>30</u>	19<u>80</u> 19<u>81</u>	19<u>81</u> 19<u>82</u>	19__ 19__	19__ 19__	19__ 19__	19__ 19__	19__ 19__
Subjects/Marking Period			1 2 3 4	1 2 3 4						
Reading			C C C C	D D G-C	B B-C					
Spelling			C B C C	C C-C C	C+ B B					
Penmanship			C C D C	G+ C C C	C+ C					
Language					C B C+B					
Mathematics			B B B+B	B- B B-B	C C C+C					
Social Studies (geog.)			B B+B+B	C B B B	B B-B					
Science			B B+A-B	A A B	B+B B					
Art/Music			B B B B	C C B B	C B B					
Physical Ed.			B A A B	A A A B	A-A A					
Sewing/Cooking										
Industrial Arts (shop)										

87

SAMPLE PUPIL CUMULATIVE RECORD
Yearly Record: Elementary and Secondary School—Intelligence Tests

Group and Individual Intelligence Tests

Group								Individual								
Grade	Date	Name of Test	Form	V	NV	IQ	%tile	Grade	Date	Name of Test	Form	CA	MA	VIQ	PIQ	IQ	%tile
3	2/80	Otis-Lennon				114	81										

Key to abbreviations: V—Verbal; NV—Nonverbal; IQ—IQ score; %tile—Percentile; CA—Chronological Age; MA—Mental Age; VIQ—Verbal IQ; PIQ—Performance IQ; IQ—Overall IQ; %tile—Percentile.

Reading—Subtests assess reading comprehension, vocabulary, and word-study skills

Math—Subtests assess math concepts, computation, and application.

1. We see from the achievement test record that Tony has performed in an overall consistent manner each time he took the test.
2. The one possible exception is in his area of strength, mathematics. Here his scores have decreased. We might want to follow up on this decrease to see if his low overall reading skills may be interfering with such tasks as application of mathematical knowledge in word problems.
3. We know from his group intelligence test score of 114 that Tony has good overall ability and this would again cause us to ask why his reading achievement scores are not higher.

We hope these examples will help parents to read their children's school records. They are as important to understand as your bank book or your salary check, because these are the records the school uses to evaluate your child's progress. Now that you have the right of access to your child's records, read them carefully and correctly. Check all the information for accuracy. (Yes, school records contain errors as do all records.) Make copies to take home, if you can do so without creating a scene. (Be sure to pay for the school's copy machine services!)

Above all, read them correctly and keep your own record of them.

CHAPTER 8

John and Sheila and Henry and Vicki: Four Individual Children

John: A Problem with Mathematics or Missed Instruction?

John is in the fifth grade in a local public elementary school. He has been doing fine in school, except in mathematics where his teacher reports that he seems to lack comprehension of mathematical concepts. As a pupil she reports John to be cooperative, helpful, and a good citizen in the classroom. He seems to try hard in mathematics but he just takes so much longer than the other children. He doesn't really seem to comprehend what is going on even when she gives him after school help. When John's parents come to school, they are very concerned since John worries about his mathematics at home and thinks he is "dumb" at it.

John's scores on the test records show that his IQ score is 121, which puts him in the upper quarter of his school population and at the 90th percentile. His reading scores show him to be about the middle of the seventh grade level with a percentile rank of 56, which makes him about two years ahead in reading and spelling. His social studies score is also up at the beginning of the seventh grade equivalent level or 80th percentile and science is at the sixth grade equivalent and the 42nd percentile. But, mathematics was at 3.6 placing him at the 12th percentile when John was tested in the fifth grade, third month. John's parents and the teacher looked at these test results and wondered if John was one of those youngsters who just has difficulty with mathematics. John's parents felt that his scores were uniformly high and consistent with his IQ score, except for mathematics. They wondered why his mathematics scores were low.

PARENTS: Do you think that John has a special problem with mathematics and just has trouble learning it?

TEACHER: I don't know. It certainly looks that way. What does he say at home?

PARENTS: He says that the work is hard for him and he doesn't understand it. When we try to help him, we can see he doesn't understand how to do some of these word problems at all.

TEACHER: John is new to the school this year. Do you remember how he did last year in mathematics?

PARENTS: Let me see. Last year John moved in the middle of the year, but he was doing all right in the fall. In the spring the teacher said that he was a little bit behind, but we don't remember much trouble with it.

TEACHER: You said John moved in the middle of the year. Has he had several moves?

PARENTS: Oh yes. Doesn't the record show it there? John had been in five schools by the time he was entering the fifth grade. We have had to move around a great deal. He had a year in the Middle East where we were stationed. It was an English-speaking school, but I don't know what he was taught in mathematics there.

TEACHER: It could be a real problem if John has had lots of different kinds of mathematics instruction. Mathematics, as you know, is the one subject in which you must have instruction. In reading, children can go on and read on their own, once they have mastered the basic skills. But in mathematics children have to be taught the next step. Only a few prodigies can figure out these next steps by themselves. Do you have any idea what books he used in mathematics in other schools?

PARENTS: No, he had a red book in one, I know, and a blue book in another, and some workbooks he brought home, but I don't recall the names of them.

TEACHER: What I think we should do, based on what you've been telling us, is some diagnostic work with John and see where the holes are. I suspect that he has had many different forms of instruction. He is probably mixed up on some of the basic mathematical skills.

PARENTS: That seems like a good idea.

TEACHER: Do you know, for example, whether or not he has mastered the multiplication table?

PARENTS: No, we don't know. But I think he has trouble with it sometimes. I've seen him counting on his fingers to do a problem.

TEACHER: I think we should move right into a diagnostic assessment of his mathematical skills. I think we are going to find he has some real holes in his basic learning, with all this moving around.

PARENTS: Suppose we find that out. Then what do we do?

TEACHER: What I think we do is see that he gets some extra instruction to make up for it. I think there's nothing wrong with John except that he's missed some instruction.

It is astonishing how often teachers and parents miss lack of instruction as a cause of a learning problem! One such cause can be moving around, as parents and families do these days. The result is that the child is exposed to one type of curriculum, then another, and often the sequence gets jumbled so that the children can miss completely one particular part of instruction. The sequence is crucial in mathematics which requires instruction for progress. Children on their own simply cannot figure out fractions, decimals, and how to do word problems. The same thing can happen if the child has been ill and has missed a great deal of school, and consequently missed a good deal of instruction. When we see a pattern of a child who is an able learner and has uniformly good achievement across all subjects except one, and if this subject is mathematics, the problem may be lack of instruction, not lack of mathematical ability. It is true that some children really do have a lot of problems with mathematics and need extra instruction in it, but before making that judgment, one should check out the amount of instruction and the consistency of it.

Sheila: Underachiever or Slow Learner in This School?

Sheila is in the seventh grade and is a very attractive, sociable girl who is popular with her classmates and a student whom the teacher feels is a real asset to the classroom. She is attentive in class, responsible, has very nice manners, and has a way of soothing disagreements among her classmates. Sheila is the kind of girl that everybody likes and who has a great deal of social skill with her peers and with adults. She has always been an attractive child. Teachers from nursery school on have always liked her. Sheila is the first child in her family with a brother who is a good deal younger, to whom she is devoted. Her parents say she is a wonderful sister to him and he, in turn, is devoted to her. He just entered kindergarten this year.

Sheila's parents have become concerned about her this year for the first time. She seems to worry about her school work a lot and acts discouraged about it, even teary-eyed, which is a change. She has always been a happy child, with lots of friends and enjoyed school. This year she says the work is hard for her and that she thinks she is stupid. She spends long hours on her homework, so much so that her parents must order her to bed to get some rest.

The parents have asked the guidance counselor for a conference because of their concern about her. The school has not expressed concern, although her marks from the first report period were one B, three C's and a D, which is lower than she has been getting. In elementary school up to the sixth grade, she was a B student and had an occasional A.

COUNSELOR: We want you to know how much we think of Sheila. She is a great addition to the seventh grade and all of her teachers think highly of her.

PARENTS: We appreciate that and certainly she is the same way with us, but we are concerned about her. She does not seem to enjoy school and she comes home kind of blue. She says the work is hard for her.

COUNSELOR: Do you think she is having a reaction to the change in entering junior high school?

PARENTS: Well, it certainly came with this year, it's true, with the move into the seventh grade.

COUNSELOR: Is there anything you think she is worrying about? Is there something at home that is on her mind?

PARENTS: No, not that we can think of. Sheila gets along very well with her brother and with us. She is really a delight to have at home. But we are worrying about her. She seems to be blue too much of the time. She can't play with her friends on the weekends because she has so much homework to do. She is quite popular with the other girls and gets a lot of calls over the weekend. We would like to see her have some social life, not just be tied to her books. And then she was very upset about the report card, particularly that D in science.

COUNSELOR: Well, we often have low marks in that first marking period of the seventh grade. You know it is a time of great change for the students coming into the big building, classes in different parts of the building, a problem with more homework, and more challenging work too.

PARENTS: Yes, we hear that from other parents. Sheila is our first child so we haven't been through this with another youngster. But it seems to us that her reaction is so different from the way it was in the other grades. The marks are down too. We have a very discouraged young girl on our hands, which concerns us.

COUNSELOR: Well, I don't blame you. I would be concerned too if it were my youngster.

PARENTS: Do you have any information that could help us understand what is going on?

COUNSELOR: Let me see her records. She had an IQ test in the first grade when she tested at 115, and her achievement test scores were about grade level—no, they were above grade level in third grade. I see they slipped a little bit in fifth grade. She went down in her reading comprehension there a little bit. She was a little bit behind grade in that. However, I would say average or a little bit below average for fifth grade in this system.

PARENTS: That seems kind of odd to us. Sheila has always gotten good marks all through grade school and we really did have no idea she was below grade in anything.

COUNSELOR: Well, it is not a big difference. I notice her reading comprehension was about a year behind at fifth grade.

PARENTS: Well, if you look at her report card, you'll see she was getting B, B+, and A all through elementary school. We never heard a word of concern from the school about her at all.

COUNSELOR: Well, apparently she did quite well or she wouldn't have been getting those grades. Of course she is an awfully nice youngster.

PARENTS: Yes, but we feel we would like to know if there is any problem with her work. What does the score in reading comprehension mean?

COUNSELOR: It is her ability to understand what she reads, and her rate of reading.

PARENTS: Does that mean she has a reading block or she has some problem in reading skills?

COUNSELOR: No, it doesn't. Her reading skills are quite good judging from her grades in first and second grade. Reading comprehension is really a matter of intelligence more than anything else, the ability to comprehend what one reads.

PARENTS: Well, how bright is Sheila? I don't think we've ever been told her IQ.

COUNSELOR: I think I mentioned she had an IQ score of 115 in elementary school.

PARENTS: Well, can that change over time? Does that mean we should have another test now?

COUNSELOR: Well, we could have an individual intelligence test if you would like to have that done. I'm sure we could arrange it. But I'm sure she is an able girl and what she needs to do really is to get a little bit more help with that science or maybe get one of the older students here to tutor her.

Shortly after this conversation, Sheila was tested by a school psychologist and found to have a full IQ score of 98 with a performance score of 110 and a verbal score of 93. Her parents found that, for Sheila, comprehending words was a much more difficult task than it was for other children of her age in that school system. The drop in reading comprehension in fifth grade probably reflected the fact that she was not as quick a learner verbally as the other children and was not learning as much from what she read. When Sheila got to seventh grade in junior high, she found the work increasingly difficult and found science in particular to be difficult. The kind of science she was studying was very demanding at a conceptual and abstract level, which Sheila could not handle. Sheila, who was so skillful in her social relationships and so pleasant and responsible in elementary school, was always viewed by her teachers as a good student who worked hard and who was conscientious. Probably as a result Sheila got somewhat more favorable marks from her teachers than her actual performance deserved. As time went on, and the school work became more difficult, Sheila's relatively slower rate of learning became more apparent, particularly when she confronted the more complex and abstract materials associated with junior high school. Her parents were quite surprised initially with her IQ of 98 when they felt she was 115. The school psychologist had to spend a good deal of time explaining to the parents how test results can change with the type of test, and how 98, although within the average range, is a handicap when one is competing with children in a particular system whose average IQ was around 110.

Sheila's parents were very sensible. They immediately readjusted their expectations for her, realizing that school learning and verbal learning were not going to be easy for her, but that she would always be very talented in dealing with people and would be considered by others to be a very desirable friend and member of any social group. With the help of the counselor they lightened her load and planned a lighter load for her through junior high. Sheila was switched to a different science section which was more concrete and less abstract. Sheila reacted very well to a lightened load, was able to spend more time in recreation on the weekend which was important to her, and made a very good adjustment.

Henry: Learning Disability or Brain Dysfunction?

Henry is a small boy in third grade, smaller than the rest of his classmates. He has a kind of owlish look about him and on the playground he is chosen last for any kind of running game. He is not well coordinated and his writing is very painful to watch. He grasps the pencil between his fingers as though he is going to choke it to death. What he writes is very hard to read, for Henry and everyone else. His teacher thinks of Henry as being immature and has written this on the descriptive report card that goes home. She says that he doesn't pay attention in class and sometimes cries when the other boys pick on him. He is having trouble with reading, trouble with his writing, his spelling is almost impossible to follow, but his mathematics is at grade level. His parents have been worried about him right along. They regard him as immature also. He has an older brother who is in sixth grade who gets along well in school and is achieving well. Henry has been seen recently by the school psychologist who has completed an evaluation and is now meeting with Henry's parents.

SCHOOL PSYCHOLOGIST: Henry shows a somewhat unusual picture on the WISC-R, the Wechsler Intelligence Scale for Children. He has a very low verbal IQ score and a very high performance IQ score which together show him overall to be about 105 IQ at this age.

PARENTS: What does this low verbal, high performance mean?

SCHOOL PSYCHOLOGIST: I don't know what it means, but we see it in a certain proportion of children, often in boys like this when we get a very uneven performance. Some people think that the organism is young and not yet caught up with its verbal maturity as compared to its performance. Some people would call it a learning disability perhaps. Other people think it is a differential rate of growth of the brain and would probably think that Henry shows some signs of what some people would call a brain dysfunction with his poor coordination and his immature behavior. However, my own view is Henry is indeed immature, and we have simply overlooked the fact that he is a lot younger than most of the children in his grade. Henry has a December birthdate, you know, and that means he is competing with children who on the average are six months or older than he is, which is a big difference at this age.

PARENTS: Yes, that is true. He is young and he has always been young in his class. When we moved here just before first grade, they tested him and said that they felt he was ready for first grade, so we let him go in. He had had two years of nursery and kindergarten in the other school. As we look at it now, we wish we had held him back.

SCHOOL PSYCHOLOGIST: I wish you had too. That's something we almost always recommend, that it is better for a youngster to be more mature for his grade than be more immature, particularly when he is first starting school. But that has been done. Now we have the problem of Henry being in the third grade and being young. He does act younger than the other children and of course they see that as being babyish. I've noticed on the playground that he plays more often with second graders than third graders.

PARENTS: Yes, that is true on the block too. His best friends are younger than he is.

SCHOOL PSYCHOLOGIST: Too bad we can't rewrite history and just move his birthdate up a year, isn't it?

PARENTS: Yes, that would be a marvelous solution!

SCHOOL PSYCHOLOGIST: Now we have him here, in the third grade, and having problems learning many of these skills.

PARENTS: What do you think we should do? Do you think he needs extra help or what?

SCHOOL PSYCHOLOGIST: I think he needs some extra help, but I also think we need time. Many of these youngsters seem to get better as they get older without special handling. I think we should get him extra help, and I think then we should consider the possibility of either putting him on a very heavy tutoring program in fourth grade to help make up for some of these things he is missing, or else keeping him in third grade next year.

PARENTS: Oh, we'd hate to keep him back! It would be so embarrassing and so hard for him!

SCHOOL PSYCHOLOGIST: Yes, that is a problem, but we have to weigh that against the possibility of putting him into the fourth grade as a young child, into the fifth grade as a young child, into the sixth grade as a young child, and asking him to play "catch up ball" for the next years of his life.

PARENTS: Yes. That's true. But isn't it awfully hard on youngsters to keep them back?

SCHOOL PSYCHOLOGIST: Yes, it's hard on them at first, but it doesn't last forever. If the youngster can do better in that grade, it does a lot for them in their own sense of confidence.

PARENTS: What if we have him tutored this summer?

SCHOOL PSYCHOLOGIST: That's one thing that could be done. I think you have to weigh that against what your plans are for this summer and Henry's need to have some fun too. If it's done well and done with some enjoyment, I think it might help to keep his skills up before the fourth grade. We could try it and see, and then reassess him just before school begins. We can make the decision in August about the right grade placement.

PARENTS: We have a friend who is said to be a very good tutor and who lives on the same block. I was wondering if we could arrange to have her work with him every day in the morning. Then he could be free to play or go to day camp for part of the summer, or something like that.

SCHOOL PSYCHOLOGIST: That seems like a good plan if he gets along well with her and she can see him on a regular basis. The regularity of tutoring and the frequency makes a difference.

PARENTS: We can certainly look into that. What do you think about the future? Is Henry going to be like this all his life?

SCHOOL PSYCHOLOGIST: It has been my experience that these youngsters change over time and settle down a great deal. It has also been my experience that they take after somebody in the family very often. Is there anybody in the family that was like this early on?

PARENTS: Well, I think he is a bit the way his father was.

SCHOOL PSYCHOLOGIST: It's not unusual. Tell me what Henry was like when he was younger.

PARENTS: Well, he was a youngster that didn't want to go to bed at night and didn't want to sleep. Compared to his older brother he was a pea on a hot griddle and into everything. When he was young we nicknamed him "monkey" because he was up and down and in and around and into things and pulling things apart. My goodness, he was a handful!

SCHOOL PSYCHOLOGIST (TO THE FATHER): Were you like that when you were young?

FATHER: They say I was. My mother says I was a real handful and I never went to sleep at all. I kept them up at all hours. She said that if I had been the first she never would have had another one!

SCHOOL PSYCHOLOGIST: Did that change for you at some point? Obviously it must have.

FATHER: Yes, it did. I think I was very much like Henry when I was in the early grades. They say I was. I was lucky though that I wasn't young for my grade. I was a year behind in a sense. But as I got older, I guess I grew out of some of that. I wouldn't rave about my handwriting today and I guess I am a lot more active than a lot of people. For example, I don't like to sit through a meeting. I have to get up and walk around.

People say I am sort of a jumpy type and I have to move quickly. One reason why I like my business is that I get to move around a lot. I'm in real estate. I don't think I could stand a job where I'd have to sit at a desk from 9 to 5. It would just drive me up a wall! But I really like my work and I think I am good at it. But what do you think about Henry? Do you think he's always going to have a problem in school?

SCHOOL PSYCHOLOGIST: No, I don't think so. But I think he will have a problem during this period, until we either get him into his own age group or give him enough extra instruction to help him catch up. I would hate to burden him with all this extra work at this point. In some ways I think it might be wiser to lighten his load and put him back with people who are closer to his level of maturity. If you are reluctant to make that decision now, we can decide at the end of the summer.

PARENTS: Is it possible that he has a learning disability?

SCHOOL PSYCHOLOGIST: Well, some people might call it that. My view is that we are dealing with a child who is immature across the board, is having trouble across most of his subjects in most of the basic skills. He seems to be talented in mathematics, which is good. But he is having trouble in reading, writing, spelling, and in all those early skills. I think it is probably not out of line with his level of maturity. In other words if you look at him being as young as he really is—forget his birthday and think of him as a year younger—he is really not doing badly at all. He is struggling to keep up with children who are a good deal older than he is in neurological development and in their conceptual development. If we give him the right kind of pacing, I think we will see an improvement in him in this grade without any help. I think things will get worse and worse for him if we don't do that.

The parents were reluctant to accept the idea of holding Henry in the third grade, but by the end of the summer, after reassessment, they were convinced that it would be too hard for him to go into the fourth grade. Henry repeated third grade, which was only partially successful, but he was able to hold his own by repeating. His behavior seemed much more normal for children of that age than for children in the older age group. He was also given extra reading help. By the end of the third (repeated) grade, Henry was at grade level in reading, even though his handwriting and spelling were still a problem. By sixth grade his handwriting was legible and Henry seemed to have taken a big jump in maturity. He was still a quick-moving child and couldn't sit still for long, but he had stopped being babyish and was considered a normal member of the classroom.

Vicki: Motivation or a Block?

Vicki is a tenth grader whose teachers report her as lacking motivation. Vicki has an IQ score of 116 as of ninth grade and her aptitude test scores suggest that she should do well in high school work. Instead, Vicki is getting C's, C – 's, and D's in her five subjects. Vicki does not particularly enjoy school and often tells her mother that she wishes she were in another school. Vicki's teachers have tried everything they can think of and now have given up on her. They think she just doesn't try hard enough. Vicki doesn't turn in homework assignments, she sometimes says she lost the papers, and she failed to turn in a term paper. This kind of behavior antagonizes her teachers who feel that she just doesn't really care.

Vicki lives with her mother but sees her father on weekends. Her mother and father were divorced last year. Her father has remarried, and his second wife has two children by her first marriage, a boy and a girl aged seven and nine who are living with them. Both Vicki's mother and father live in the same town, although in different areas of the town. Vicki's mother has had to go to work as a consequence of the divorce, and is also going to night school in an attempt to upgrade her credentials. Vicki has always been a responsible girl, well mannered, and not a problem to her parents. She is well liked in school and has a number of friends, none of whom are in trouble at school or out of school. She is moderately attractive but has no regular boyfriend. Vicki would like to get a job but has not been able to find one. Her mother feels that it is too much for Vicki to do, and is very discouraged about Vicki's present status in school. Her father is quite upset about it. Vicki's mother comes to have a talk with the school psychologist who had been seeing Vicki about her attitude toward school.

SCHOOL PSYCHOLOGIST: I am delighted you could come in. As you know, I've seen Vicki just twice because she came to see me on her own, to say she was very unhappy in school and disliked being here.
VICKI'S MOTHER: She told me that she had come. Of course I am very concerned about her. The marks really are not like Vicki. She has always been a very responsible youngster. Even though she has not been an A student, she's always been a B and C student.
SCHOOL PSYCHOLOGIST: Yes, I know. I was looking at her record just the other day and I have it here. It's clear her marks have gone down in the past year or so. Do you have any notion why that is?
VICKI'S MOTHER: Well, I suppose the divorce is part of the picture. I think she took it kind of hard. She's very fond of her father and now he's remarried. Now she sees him on weekends and as far as I know that goes well. She tells me it goes well anyhow.
SCHOOL PSYCHOLOGIST: I understand you are working and trying to get your life back together.
VICKI'S MOTHER: Yes, I am. I'm working at the bank and then I am taking courses three evenings a week to try to get myself retrained. It's been a long time since I've been at work and it's kind of hard to get back in.

SCHOOL PSYCHOLOGIST: Yes, I know it is hard and I think you have a lot of courage to tackle what you are doing. It must be an awfully tough schedule for you, isn't it?

VICKI'S MOTHER: Yes, it is hard. It really is. I try to get Vicki off in the morning and we have breakfast together. But then I get home around 5 and it's hard sometimes to get supper together and get over to school around 7. That's three nights a week you know. And I am tired from taking care of the house. Vicki does help me, but it doesn't leave much time for fun, and I don't think I am very good company for Vicki, to tell you the truth. It seems to me that there is so much to be done sometimes. I'm so tired, I really just fall into bed when I get back from school.

SCHOOL PSYCHOLOGIST: I am sure you must be tired. It must be a difficult schedule and I don't suppose there is much fun in it for you. What about Vicki?

VICKI'S MOTHER: Well, I don't think being home is all that much fun for her either. Sometimes we have supper together, and sometimes we don't, and then of course I'm gone. About the only time we have to see each other is on the weekend and then Vicki is over with her father, and I don't feel I'd like to interfere with that. I think Vicki has the right to be with her father.

SCHOOL PSYCHOLOGIST: Does she enjoy going over there on weekends, do you think?

VICKI'S MOTHER: She says she does to me, but maybe she has told you what she really thinks?

SCHOOL PSYCHOLOGIST: She hasn't said too much about that, but I get the impression that it isn't always as good as it might be. I think her father is pretty much wrapped up in this new marriage and with those two new children to raise. I suspect Vicki might feel like a fifth wheel in that household.

VICKI'S MOTHER: Yes, I suppose that's true. I hadn't thought about it that way. I suppose that is true at home too. I am dating someone. I don't know how serious it will be but I do go out one or sometimes two nights a week. I think Vicki likes him. She says she does.

SCHOOL PSYCHOLOGIST: She told me about him. She said she thought he was quite nice, but she hoped you wouldn't remarry.

VICKI'S MOTHER: Well, I have no intention of remarrying for a long, long time. That certainly is not in the picture at all.

SCHOOL PSYCHOLOGIST: Do you think Vicki knows that or does she think you're about to get married again?

VICKI'S MOTHER: I don't think she thinks that. But of course I could make it clear to her.

SCHOOL PSYCHOLOGIST: I was thinking about your schedule and how little fun there is in it. I got to thinking about Vicki's schedule and how it must be for her. Now she comes home from school and I guess you get home around 5, and then you both have supper and then what happens?

VICKI'S MOTHER: On the nights I have to go back to class, she is very good about it. She will clean up after me and then I will get in around 9:30. Of course I am pretty tired and I tend to go to bed right away.

SCHOOL PSYCHOLOGIST: Yes, I am sure you are. I was thinking in terms of Vicki's life. There really isn't much fun in it for her. You are obviously overburdened right now and her father is busy with his new marriage, and I wonder if Vicki doesn't feel as if she is left out of things?

VICKI'S MOTHER: I never looked at it that way. Life really isn't much fun for Vicki either. It is really rather grim around our house. Money is a problem for us and Vicki has offered to work, but I don't think she should. Do you? What I said was that this is my responsibility and I am going to see to it that while she is in school she can have her free time and have her fun.

SCHOOL PSYCHOLOGIST: I guess that depends on how you see fun. It seems to me that Vicki is not having all that much fun now. She might be the kind of youngster who is better off sharing the responsibility with you. Maybe Vicki feels a little bit left out of that too. Maybe she would really enjoy going to work and feeling that she is helping to carry the load with you.

VICKI'S MOTHER: Perhaps. But I really don't want her going to work. I went to work when I was very young and we had a rough time. I feel that while Vicki is in high school I will try to see that she doesn't work. I hope to be able to manage some college for her with her father's help.

SCHOOL PSYCHOLOGIST: Perhaps one thing you should do is talk over the possibility of Vicki going to work. If she feels strongly about helping out that way, I am sure she could manage it.

VICKI'S MOTHER: But won't her marks go down even more?

SCHOOL PSYCHOLOGIST: Well, I don't see that as all so much of a problem. She is not doing all that well now and clearly not putting in that much time studying. If she had a definite time to go to work, maybe she would use her time better.

VICKI'S MOTHER: I don't know, I'm just not that sure about that. I just don't want to give her too much responsibility so young.

SCHOOL PSYCHOLOGIST: I don't think we would want to burden her with too much responsibility. But right now it seems to me that Vicki is not having too much fun in life, and she feels like she doesn't belong to anyone. She seems to be the kind of person who wants to share the responsibility with you, so maybe we need to give her a chance to be a part of the team, so to speak.

Vicki's mother did talk with Vicki and they decided on a trial of letting Vicki work after school. Vicki, with encouragement from the school psychologist, was able to get a job after school in the local stationery store. Vicki proved to be an excellent worker and was encouraged by the people with whom she worked, who thought her a very fine young person. The opportunity then offered itself for her to work in the store on

Saturdays and Vicki chose to do that, rather than visit her father's family every weekend. She gradually spent more and more time with her mother and less time with her father, and that summer worked full-time in the stationery store. Her grades picked up and even a smile was occasionally seen on her face. By the end of eleventh grade she was given increased responsibility at the stationery store, where she became the owner's right-hand person. She was getting B's and C's in junior year and saving money for college.

These four children—John, Sheila, Henry, and Vicki—are four individual pupils, who each had their own sort of adjustment to school. By *no* means do we mean to imply that all children should fit into these four! What we do mean to imply is that each child has his own kind of school adjustment. The conscientious parent and school staff member will look at all the information about each youngster, at all the test scores, and at all the school records, before forming any kind of impression as to where the youngster needs help and how best to give it to that child. The four individuals we have discussed are examples of how pupils can be helped with a judicious look at the facts, which in each case means paying close attention to the records of test scores before forming any judgment about a child's ability to do better in school.

From the examples of John, Sheila, Henry, and Vicki, we can see that school records and tests helped parents and teachers understand and plan for their children. John's school record helped us understand that his many school changes may have contributed to holes in his learning of mathematics. His test scores showed that he had the ability to succeed with mathematics instruction.

In the case of Sheila, a cooperative and pleasant child, her sudden drop in grades in seventh grade caused her parents and counselor to review her record together and reassess her level of ability. Her IQ score, when compared to other children with whom she was grouped, indicated that she was in over her head and that her schedule needed to be readjusted to lighten her load.

Henry, we discovered, was a very young child for his class. His overall immaturity placed him at a great disadvantage. Testing helped determine that he was a child of average ability who might be helped, first by tutoring, and if this did not work, by repeating a grade so that he would be competing with children of his own age.

Vicki's above average scores on an intelligence test helped her mother and the school psychologist understand that her low grades in school were a result of motivation rather than of ability.

CHAPTER 9

What Are Preschool and Readiness Tests?

It is the purpose of this chapter to describe when testing is likely to occur for the young child, and to indicate the kinds of assessment procedures likely to take place.

The preschool and early school years are years when great learning and development take place with the young child. Three-, four- and five-year-old children are learning to express themselves through language; to explore the world around them; to be curious about objects and events; to play with other children; and to develop greater motor coordination and facility in manipulating objects. They are also developing readiness for reading, arithmetic, and for following the routines they will encounter in the classroom. Along with parents, educators and psychologists have increasingly recognized the importance of the preschool years in the child's development. Headstart, day-care, and nursery school programs have dedicated their efforts to developing the abilities of young children from different backgrounds. Educators concerned with helping children with special needs have focused increased attention on the very young child. Both federal and state funds have been channeled to the preschool level with the hope of preventing later school difficulty. Given this interest, it is not surprising that testing of the young child prior to first grade has received increased attention.

When children enter nursery school, Headstart, or day-care programs, the teachers, aides, day-care workers, and others caring for them will be observing and interacting with them. These persons will be learning what each child enjoys, will try, is sensitive to, and what he or she can do. They will see day-to-day changes and will encourage each child to engage in new and different experiences, as well as familiar and pleasur-

Expressive language	Child's ability to produce words and sentences which include nouns, verbs, adjectives, and prepositions to express themselves (child expresses the words = expressive)
Speech	Child's ability to produce words and sounds correctly

Cognitive

Concepts	Child's ability to understand and follow concepts such as "same," "fast," "happy," and "more" which are used in directions
Comprehension	Understanding the meaning of words, such as "a fork is used for cutting" and "an umbrella is used when it rains"
Relationships	Ability to see that things are connected so that a child understands that a cup goes with a saucer
Classification	Ability to group together things of a kind such as things we wear or things we eat

Adaptive

Personal-social	Child's ability to interact and play with other children, as well as to follow normal routines
Self-help	Ability to take care of self and manage without help such as putting on clothing and going to the toilet unassisted

Screening Tests and Procedures

As noted earlier, screening tests will be used to help identify those skills children already possess as well as those areas that need development in the cognitive, language, physical motor, and personal-social areas.

Some examples of screening tests are given here.

SCREENING TESTS

Name	Age	What It Measures
Cognitive Skills Assessment Battery (CSAB) (Boehm and Slater)	Pre-K–K	Screens for child's level of understanding relative to teaching goals in the areas: orientation toward the environment, ability to see similarities and differences, comprehension and concept formation, coordination, and memory

SCREENING TESTS (Continued)

Name	Age	What It Measures
Denver Developmental Screening Test (Frankenburg, Dodds, et al.)	1 mo.– 6 years	Screens for significant delays in the social, language, gross, and fine motor areas.
McCarthy Screening Test (McCarthy)	2½– 8½ years	Screens for children likely to meet difficulty with school work. Based on the comprehensive McCarthy Scale.
Meeting Street School Screening Test (Hainsworth and Siqueland)	K–1	Screens to identify children with possible language, visual-motor or gross-motor problems that could interfere with learning.
The Preschool Inventory (Caldwell)	3–6 years	Screens across areas seen as necessary for success in school such as basic information and vocabulary; size, shape, color, time, and number concepts; visual-motor functioning; following directions and self-help skills.

Closely related to these tests are developmental scales. Developmental scales are based on observation of the child's behavior and skill as they develop. The child's development is compared with the typical development of children of the same age and sometimes of the same sex, since the rate of development of boys and girls is different. Some examples of developmental scales are given here.

DEVELOPMENTAL SCALES

Name	Age	What It Measures
Bayley Scales of Infant Development (Bayley)	2–30 months	Development of young children assessed in three major areas—mental, motor, and infant behavior
The Pupil Rating Scale Revised (Myklebust)	5–14 years	Screening for possible learning disabilities. Ratings are made by teachers across the areas of comprehending word meanings, following instructions, comprehending class discussions, memory and motor coordination.
Vineland Social Maturity Scale (Doll)	Birth–30 years	Based on parent interview, the scale helps rate the child's competence with self-help behaviors, abilities to communicate and to socialize with others.
Preschool Attainment Record (PAR)(Doll)	6 mos. – 7 years	An extension of the *Vineland Social Maturity Scale* and measures the same areas.

Screening and the use of developmental scales often takes place as a regular part of a school program. Its end is not to label or classify children, but to assist teachers in planning meaningful learning experiences for them. If, through screening, a learning problem is suspected, a child is then referred to the school psychologist or "learning disabilities team" (called by different labels in different locations) for more in-depth evaluation or diagnosis. Parent involvement is most important here, as well as early records of the child's development, indication of unusual incidents, accidents, or illnesses, and general impressions about the child.

Readiness Testing

Readiness means the child has *mastered* the necessary *pre*-skills to benefit from formal instruction in a subject, such as reading or mathematics. Assessment is related to readiness and is carried out for at least two reasons: (1) to predict whether a child will have trouble with early reading and mathematics learning, and (2) to find out if the child has the prerequisite skills, so we can take action *before* the child is faced with the task of learning to read or to compute with numbers.

Readiness tests are generally administered to children at the beginning of kindergarten, end of kindergarten, or beginning of first grade, to help teachers identify the readiness of children to engage in the formal learning tasks of reading and mathematics. Directions on readiness tests are read aloud to children who select and mark a picture or write letters and numbers asked for by the teacher. In most cases children practice activities before taking the tests to make sure they can follow the directions and are familiar with the procedures required. For example, test questions might be included such as: "Mark the picture that begins with the same sound as *dog*," or "Mark the picture that shows three stars."

What are some of the prerequisite skills the child needs? Among the skills assessed by many readiness measures are:

1. Discrimination of letters and numbers (which is different from naming them). For example, can the child identify the letter b in the group of letters g s b w, or the number 5 in the group of numbers 3 5 8 2?
2. Matching letters, numbers, letter sequences, or words to a sample such as "Find the letter that is just like the one (letter) in the box." $\boxed{\text{p}}$ d   r   p   s
3. Auditory discrimination, such as "Look at the letters in the box and listen to me. Now find the letter that matches the sound that I say."

   "t" $\boxed{\text{d   s   p   t}}$
4. Picture recognition, such as "mark the chair."

5. Listening comprehension, such as the child's ability to understand simple stories.
6. Association of number symbols to groups of objects, such as

   5

7. Quantitative concepts such as "Mark the biggest ball."

Some commonly used readiness tests are listed here.

READINESS TESTS

Name	Age	What It Measures
Comprehensive Test of Basic Skills (CTB/McGraw Hill)	K–1	Measures skill mastery in language and mathematics.
Metropolitan Readiness Tests (MRT) (Nurss & McGauvran)	K–1	Assesses child's understanding of consonants, sound-letter correspondence, matching of letters, numbers and shapes; finding patterns hidden in other pictures; vocabulary, comprehension, and understanding numbers.
Stanford Early School Achievement Test (SEAT) (Madden & Gardner)	K–1	Assesses child's information about his/her environment, mathematics, letters and sounds, listening comprehension, reading words and sentences (at grade 1 only)
Peabody Picture Vocabulary Test (PPVT) (Dunn & Dunn)	2½–Adult	Assesses receptive language, that is the child's ability to identify pictures that correspond to spoken directions

Many of these tests at the preschool level actually measure general learning efficiency or readiness. The assumption underlying many of these tests is that the greater the understanding the child has picked up from daily exposure to life experiences that relate to early reading and mathematics, the greater the *readiness* to deal with related school learning tasks. Tests, however, do not assess all of what children know. Since there are many changes from day to day in the behavior of young children, tests do not do a perfect job in assessing readiness. The kindergarten teacher who observes the day-to-day behavior of children can provide important insights as to which children will have difficulty or ease with later learning tasks. Therefore, teacher ratings need to be used along with information gained from tests in making readiness decisions.

Tests of Specific and General Learning Skills

In contrast to those tests which measure reading readiness or mathematics readiness specifically, tests have been developed to help teachers assess children's mastery of concepts and skills associated with early learning in general, again to assist in planning early learning experiences. Some examples of these tests, which can be given any time during the school year, are given here.

BASIC SKILLS TESTS

Name	Age	What It Measures
Boehm Test of Basic Concepts (BTBC) (Boehm)	5–7	Child's understanding of basic relational concepts such as "top," "same," and "first" which are important to school learning
Brigance Diagnostic Inventory of Basic Skills (Brigance)	K–6	Child's readiness and skill level across subject areas covered in the elementary school: readiness, reading, language, arts, and mathematics
CIRCUS (Anderson, Bogatz, Draper, et al.)	Pre-K–1	Assesses children's understanding and performance across 17 learning areas to plan instruction. Among the areas covered are seeing similarities and differences, problem solving, and story comprehension
Tests of Basic Experiences 2 (TOBE-2) (Moss)	Pre-K–1	Assesses child's understanding and awareness of concepts and skills across four areas: mathematics, language, science, and social studies to help in planning instruction

These tests may result in an overall score or scores telling how children performed on each item. Their purpose is to help the teacher plan learning programs matched to the children. For example, on the *Boehm Test of Basic Concepts,* the teacher will learn which relational concepts, such as *right, left, before,* and *after,* a child knows. The planning of daily instruction can then take this information into account for individual children. Learning experiences can be planned to practice the concepts children do not know. The same is true of the *Brigance Diagnostic Inventory of Basic Skills.* This inventory can be used along with detailed teaching guides to specify learning objectives for children.

Our focus throughout this chapter thus far has been on familiarizing parents with some of the more widely used tests for young children. Much understanding regarding the behavior of young children comes through observing them in their natural setting. The nursery school teacher will observe such things as the child's ability to express himself or herself through language, to play with other children, to jump and hop, or to tell about things that are important. Such ongoing observations are vital to understanding and working with the developing child.

Parents will also be observing the growing child, noting how the child attempts new experiences, how and when new skills are developed, difficulties the child encounters, and much more. These at home observations become very important to the person working with the child. Parents who observe very special talents, abilities, or skills in their child will help the teacher make appropriate plans for their child. For example, knowing that a very silent child talks to a favorite pet at home may help the teacher understand how to draw this child out in school. Parents are often welcome to observe children in preschool settings as well.

Questions Parents Should Ask About Assessing the Preschool Child

Parents have many of the same questions as do professionals about assessing children at this age. For example, "How consistent (reliable) is assessment of the rapidly developing child?" Or, "How adequate are our current tests and procedures in providing the information we need for planning and placement of the child?" Since child behavior changes so quickly at this level, it is often difficult to determine what things are within normal expectations for a child versus what signs might be signals for real concern.

Questions parents should ask about test results at the preschool level follow.

"How Are Scores Reported? What Do They Mean?"

Scores can be reported in a number of ways including:

Indication of level of risk. Not at risk: no problems in dealing with learning tasks expected. At risk: problems in learning anticipated; special attention/observation needed.

Percentiles and item scores. For example, the child might receive a score at the 45th percentile on the mathematics subtest of the *Test of Basic Experiences*. This means that the child scored at or above 45 percent of other children the same age taking the test. Other information useful for the teacher and parents on this test is the way the child performed on each item. This information can be used in planning instruction.

On many tests at the preschool and primary grade levels, the teacher will fill out a class record sheet which might look something like the form below. You can note from the example that, while a score is presented, the major focus is on how each child performed on each item.

Item or what the item measures											
Name of Child	Item	Item	Item	Item	Item	Item	Item	Item	Item	Score	Percentile
Name											
Name											
Name											

Sentence reports. On the *CIRCUS* for example, the child's scores can be converted into sentences which can describe what the child can and cannot do. For example, see page 112.

EXAMPLE OF SCORES CONVERTED TO DESCRIPTIVE SENTENCES[1]

NURSERY SCHOOL			KINDERGARTEN			
Total score	a Compre- hension	b Interpre- tation	Total Score	a Compre- hension	b Interpre- tation	Report
23-25			24-25			Very competent in listening comprehension skills, as indicated by both comprehension and interpretation of what was said.
14-22	11-15	7-10	16-23	12-15	7-10	Generally competent in listening to a story and understanding it.
	11-15	0-6		12-15	0-6	Generally competent in listening to a story and understanding it, but did not respond correctly to many items requiring interpretive responses.
	0-10	7-10		0-11	7-10	Generally competent in listening to a story and understanding it, but did not respond correctly to many items requiring simple comprehension of what was said.
	0-10	0-6		0-11	0-6	Generally competent in listening to a story and understanding it, but probably needs further instruction and practice in some of the skills involved.
6-13	11-15	0-6	6-15	12-15	0-6	Probably needs further instruction in listening comprehension skills. Did not respond correctly to many items requiring interpretive responses.
	0-10	7-10		0-11	7-10	Probably needs further instruction in listening comprehension skills. Did not respond correctly to many items requiring simple comprehension of what was said.
	0-10	0-6		0-11	0-6	Appears to lack competence in listening comprehension skills. Probably needs further instruction and practice.
0-5			0-5			CIRCUS 9 may not have provided appropriate measurement of child's listening comprehension skills. Retesting and examination for possible hearing defects may be indicated.

[1]Circus 9, Listen to the Story, Sentence Report Table. Copyright 1978, the Educational Testing Service. Reprinted by permission.

Learning objectives.   Results from the *Brigance Diagnostic Inventory of Basic Skills* can be converted into instructional objectives such as "When presented with *(#)* colors, the child can name *(#)* correctly."

Goal area performance.   On the *Cognitive Skills Assessment Battery,* for example, the child's ability to identify shapes is one of the goal areas assessed. The child's score in this area is the number of shapes he or she can identify and name, plus the number he or she can identify but not name.

Readiness scores.   On the *Metropolitan Readiness Tests,* for example, the child's score will be translated into a readiness score that can read "Poor Risk" through "Superior" or a percentile rank.

Where Is My Child Developmentally?

Parents need to inquire about their child's areas of particular strength; areas suggesting a "developmental lag"; areas considerably below what might be expected for a child of this age; signals of possible learning difficulty. One example is the *Denver Developmental Screening Test.* This test provides helpful information by indicating whether the age at which a child can perform such tasks as using three words, is the age at which 25, 50, 75, or 90 percent of children can engage in this behavior. The child unable to do many tasks that most children of the same age can do may be displaying signals of possible learning difficulty. Since the Denver is a screening test, areas of concern need to be followed up by more thorough evaluation. Both tests and observations carried out over time help teachers and parents make decisions in this area.

What Are Some Signals of Possible Learning Difficulty?

Children with severe lags in development or outright problems in more than one of the following areas might be considered as showing signs of potential learning difficulty: speech, motor coordination, poor comprehension, difficulty in following directions, poor ability to see relations, or poor self-help skills.

What Next Steps Should I Take?

1. If the child attends school, contact the school for an appointment to express your concerns and to try to find out how you can help your child.
2. Ask about the plans that the present teacher has for working with your child.
3. Ask about what seem to be the holes where help is needed and about what special help is available.

Would Further Testing Be Advised?

First the parent might talk with teachers at school to see what might be accomplished through modifying or providing additional experiences in a systematic way in a child's program. If this does not work out, the teacher might recommend some additional testing, or the parent might decide that testing would be an important next step.

How Will the Test Scores Be Used?

When teacher observation and comments are combined with scores from readiness tests and other tests, they can be used to help the child in these ways:

1. Recommending to a parent that the child remain in nursery school or kindergarten another year so that greater development can take place before the child encounters formal instruction in reading or mathematics. This suggestion may prove particularly valuable for a boy who is among the youngest of the group.

2. Recommending to a parent that a child go into a "readiness class" or "pre-first grade," where more practice is provided in pre-reading and mathematics skills before formal instruction is started. In reality, a readiness class probably means that children will be repeating kindergarten with extra emphasis on pre-reading and mathematics skills. The difference from kindergarten is that formal reading and mathematics will be introduced as the child masters the basic skills. This extra practice and time might help some children, particularly those who are very young or seem to need extra time to grow before they will be able to cope with formal learning. However, experts do not agree on the value of just more practice and time. Some would say that the teaching of beginning reading, writing, spelling, and mathematics skills might need to be structured in different ways so that children are presented with only small amounts of learning material at one time with frequent short practice periods to help them remember and apply what they have learned.[1]

3. Providing the first grade teacher with an initial identification of the child's strength and areas needing development for planning instruction and grouping different learning areas. The teacher will regroup children as she or he observes their performance during the first grade year.

[1]See, for example, N. D. Bryant, et al., *Effects of Instructional Variables on Learning of Handicapped and Nonhandicapped Individuals* (New York: N. D. Bryant and Staff, Research Institute for the Study of Learning Disabilities, Teachers College, Columbia University, New York, N.Y., 1980).

In summary, we can see that the testing of young children can provide helpful information if it is used along with ongoing observation. The results from testing need to be used *carefully* since the young child's behavior, skills, and abilities are likely to show many changes from day to day. These changes are not necessarily reflected in test scores. It is wise to remember this maxim: the *younger* the child, the *less* that tests predict accurately.

CHAPTER 10

Testing the Child with Special Needs

Children who are gifted, or learning disabled, or physically disabled, or poor in communicating through language—all present a special challenge to the educator as well as to the parent. In this chapter, we will deal with the testing of these children with "special needs."

In 1975, Congress passed the Education for All Handicapped Children Act of 1975 (PL94-142) which requires schools to identify children likely to have learning problems. Children with specific learning disabilities have been defined by this law as:

> Those children who have a disorder in one or more of the basic psychological processes involved in understanding or in using language, spoken or written, which disorder may manifest itself in imperfect ability to listen, think, speak, read, write, spell, or do mathematical calculations. . . . (November 29, 1975)

The regulations were also designed to protect the child and to define, in part, what must go into the assessment process. Assessment of children with learning disabilities must involve:

Identifying a child's competencies as well as his or her needs

Carrying out testing in the mode of communication or language most familiar to the child

Taking into account diverse areas of functioning on the part of the child

Using the results of testing to plan learning programs which, in turn, can be implemented

The suggestions of Professor Margaret Jo Shepherd of Teachers College are acknowledged and appreciated in the preparation of this chapter.

The ultimate outcome of PL94-142 has been to help school personnel become aware of issues which affect the testing of learning handicapped children and to involve parents in testing and planning.

What Does Testing of the Child with Special Needs Involve?

As we noted in chapter 9, the goal of educators has been to increase the early identification of children with special learning needs during the earliest years of their school experience in the hope of preventing later failure.

In addition to giving their consent, parents should be involved during all phases of testing and planning for their child. Assessment steps are summarized below, along with steps parents can take.

Step 1. Preliminary   For possible   → Leads to diagnostic evalua-
         screening   problem areas   tion procedures

                        For giftedness   → Leads to testing for ability

The preliminary screening involves brief testing procedures to identify the possibility of a problem or of special ability. Here parent observations will provide needed information about the child's development. If a possible problem is suspected at screening, parents may be asked to make an appointment for diagnostic evaluation of their child. Having made the appointment and while waiting for it to take place, parents may experience some anxiety, which is quite to be expected. However, parents need to keep in mind that, while screening may suggest a problem area, an actual problem may *not* exist. During the period before the appointment, important developmental changes may be observed. Be sure to write down and report these observations when you come in for the diagnostic evaluation.

Step 2. Diagnostic   Problem areas   → Leads to planning instruc-
         testing   identified   tion, or to further evaluation
                                                and to class placement deci-
                        Giftedness   →   sions
                        assessed

Diagnostic evaluation involves comprehensive procedures with the child who has possible learning problems or giftedness. These procedures are likely to involve both an individual psychological and educational evaluation of the child, sometimes a medical examination, and a review of the child's past history both at home and at school. Parents or guardians will be interviewed during this phase of evaluation. In addition to answering questions about the development, health, and adjustment of the child, it is important for parents to add their own observations and to raise their own concerns. Since parents will have spent more time with their child than anyone else, they should be confident about their own observations. Bring in your records and snapshots of your child.

Following the diagnostic procedures, results will be reported to parents. With older children this step can help pinpoint specific difficulties such as speech, limited ability, or learning disability. This information can help parents and the diagnostic team work together in developing an appropriate program for the child. With younger children who are demonstrating signs of developmental problems the parent might be told that their child is "at risk." Being labeled "at risk," however, does not mean that problems will necessarily develop later on during the child's school career. But this label does alert parents and teachers to keep a special eye on the child. Even comprehensive diagnostic evaluation *cannot* diagnose accurately young children who will become learning disabled.

When the results of diagnostic testing are reported to parents, new or unclear terms may be used. Parents should ask to have any unclear terms defined for them. Write down these terms and their definitions.

Step 3. Program planning	Instruction is planned to match individual needs of the child, possible placement in a special class designed to serve that child's needs.

Once the child has been identified as having a learning problem, being gifted, or having a physical disability that interferes with learning, parents should participate in planning a program for their child and in its implementation. The goal with most children is to *keep them in the mainstream of the regular classroom wherever possible.*

When several alternative class placements are possible, parents may be asked to help with the decision. This choice may present a problem since parents may not have sufficient information to make a placement decision. Ask for the weekly schedule of *instruction* for each alternative; ask for the names of parents of children in each possible class placement whom you can phone for information; ask where the children are placed this year that were in each of those classes last year. Did they go back to regular class ("mainstreamed")? Did they stay in special class? What about their achievement test results?

During this stage of planning, parents may be presented with an Individualized Educational Program (IEP) for their child. The IEP spells out short-term goals for each child by the end of one academic year. The IEP will usually specify the services that are to be provided for the child; anticipated dates of the accomplishment of goals; and the procedures to be used to evaluate whether or not the goals have been accomplished. The IEP involves a great deal of information, and parents should question any item that is unclear. Various states have approached this problem in different ways. However, many states have prepared publications that explain the assessment process for the child with special needs.[1] Some states and communities have resource centers or parents organizations which provide helpful information and contact with other parents of special needs children.

Step 4. Reevaluation   Once a child has been placed in a special pro-
                          gram or is identified as being learning disabled,
                          yearly reports of progress must be made.

Parents will want to ask for specific details about their child's progress. Not only will they want to look at test results, but they need to know what specific behaviors or areas of new learning have been accomplished during the course of the school year, as compared to those stated in the IEP, and compared to the gains made by their child *before* special instruction.

Examples of Tests Used

Intelligence tests and achievement tests are used in assessment of children with special needs (see chapters 2 and 3).

Special adaptations of some widely used tests have been prepared for children who are blind or physically disabled. Special tests have also been developed specifically for handicapped children. For example, the *Hiskey-Nebraska Test of Learning Aptitude* was developed as a screening test of aptitude for both deaf and hard-of-hearing children, ages 3–16. The *Blind Learning Aptitude Test* provides a measure of learning aptitude for blind children ages 6–20.

Since many children demonstrating special needs have difficulty expressing themselves verbally, tests that do not require a verbal answer may be used in the assessment process, such as the *Peabody Picture Vocabulary Test* (PPVT) or the *Ravens Progressive Matrices* (Ravens). On the PPVT, children are presented with groups of pictures while pictured objects or situations are named by the examiner, which the child must identify from one of four possibilities presented. As the name implies, the PPVT is a vocabulary test, but it requires the child only to identify by pointing. It does not require the child to read or to respond with verbal definitions of words. This test is useful with the learning disabled child who has difficulty with reading or in expressing himself or herself through words.

[1]See, for example, *Serving the Learning Disabled Child in New York State* (Albany: University of the State of New York, NY State Education Department, Bureau of the Handicapped, Room 1069, Albany, N.Y. 12234).

The *Ravens Progressive Matrices* taps abstract thinking skills in a visual logical test. The child is presented with a series of designs from which a part is missing. The child needs to select from a group of possibilities the correct answer. Again, this task does not require the child to respond in words, but it does require the child to analyze the designs and figure out the part that is missing.

Both the PPVT and the Ravens are examples of general ability tests that can be used with children who have specific language problems.

Tests are also used which tap specific skills. Some examples are described in the following text.

Language and Speech

Some tests assess the child's ability to understand spoken words and phrases and are often referred to as tests of *receptive language,* that is, the child receives the language. Other tests will tap the child's ability to produce words and sentences and thus express himself or herself through language. These are often referred to as tests of *expressive language,* which means that the child expresses the language. Finally in this category are tests developed to assess the child's ability to produce the sounds of language, which are tests of speech or articulation. Listed below are tests of language you may encounter.

Language and Speech Tests

Name of Test	Age	What It Measures
Assessment of Children's Language Comprehension (ACLC) (Foster, Giddan, and Stark)	3–7	Child's understanding of spoken words and phrases (receptive)
Carrow Elicited Language Inventory (Carrow-Woolfolk)	3–7	Errors child makes in grammatic structure (expressive)
Goldman-Fristoe Tests of Articulation (Goldman and Fristoe)	2–above	Child's ability to reproduce the sounds of words and sentences

Visual, Motor, and Auditory Tests

The child's ability to coordinate the use of his or her body is important to success in manipulating objects and in beginning writing. Likewise the ability to see and hear will affect the ease with which learning will take place. The names of some tests in this category are included here.

Name of Test	Age	What It Measures
Bender [Visual Motor] Gestalt Test (Bender)	Preschool –above	Child's ability to reproduce a series of geometric designs which indicate visual-motor coordination
Frostig Developmental Test of Visual Perception (Frostig, Lefever, and Whittlesex)	Preschool –Grade 3	Assesses perceptual skills needed to copy figures, find hidden figures, and stay within paths
Keystone Telebinocular Battery (Keystone)	Grade 2 –above	Assesses the child's visual acuity in each eye and the use of both eyes
Berry Developmental Test of Visual-Motor Integration (Berry and Bucktenica)	2–15	Assesses possible visual and motor problems through the child's copying a series of geometric figures
Auditory Discrimination Test (Wepman)	5–8	Assesses the child's ability to discriminate whether word pairs spoken by the tester are the same or different

Social Competency and Adaptive Behavior Tests

The ability to function independently of adult help and supervision and to get along with other children and adults is important to a child's success in meeting the demands of school. The ability to function independently is of particular concern to teachers of children with limited ability. Some examples of items included on the tests in this category include putting on clothing unassisted; making change; and playing with another child without adult supervision. For the most part the tests in this category are based on an adult's observation of the child, or interview with parents. The names of some tests in this category are included here.

Name of Test	Age	What It Measures
Adaptive Behavior Scale— Public School Version (Lambert, et al.)	7–12	Child's mastery of self-help skills and interpersonal skills viewed as necessary for independence in dealing with the demands of everyday life
Cain-Levine Social Competency Scale (Cain, Levine, and Elzey)	5–13	Assesses child's competency in the areas of self-help, initiative, communication, and social skills

Questions Parents Should Ask About Their Child with Special Needs

The final section of this chapter will focus on common questions and concerns of parents of the child with special needs:

1. *What is my child's intelligence?* Parents need, first, a clear picture of their child's intelligence. Tests of intelligence for children with limitations present problems. For example, a child with a lan-

guage problem has to be tested with a nonlanguage test. Estimating intelligence from such tests may be the best data obtainable, but may be estimates at best.

2. *Is my child's intelligence higher than the test scores indicate?* Sometimes the teacher or test examiner will tell parents that their child has higher "potential" than the test scores indicate. Parents need to be *very* wary of such statements because *tests do not measure potential*—they measure current achievement only. Tests can tell us, to use an analogy, how well your child can run right now. But no test can tell us how well your child *will* run in five years, which is his or her *potential* running ability. Ask to have the child's current skills explained so that you can be aware of such areas as "listening carefully to directions" or "attention span" that might be interfering with the child's performance.

3. *Is the problem the result of poor motivation, or laziness?* It is not likely that the problem is laziness! Many children try hard, but are not able to learn as fast as other children in the class, no matter how much effort they exert. If the problem has gone by unnoticed for an extended period of time, the child may give up rather than encounter failure again, which is natural.

4. *My child is receiving D's and F's. Is this the result of poor teaching or does it suggest a learning problem?* Communicate *early* in the school year that you want to know how to help your child. Request an individual conference with the teacher and with other specialists who have seen the child. Ask about what seem to be the holes and what kind of special help is available.

   If you still have a strong basis for questioning the teacher's ability, tackle this with diplomacy initially, but come prepared. Most experts will advise parents to move slowly and carefully in challenging the quality of teaching for two reasons: (1) you do not wish to antagonize the teacher toward your child; (2) it is very hard to get any agreement on what *is* high and low quality teaching. We suggest you follow Teddy Roosevelt's advice, once you are *sure* of your facts: "Walk softly and carry a big stick." Be prepared to document any statement you make about inadequate teaching. Get other parents to join in who have made the same observations. Get a copy of the daily schedule, and count the *actual* minutes of instruction versus transportation, recess, lunch, and nonacademic activities. Request a meeting with the principal, and go to it (1) polite and (2) well prepared, which means with a plan (the big stick) for your next step if politeness does not work. Being prepared may mean working with other parents, your lawyer, the press, or the board of education. But be *sure* of your facts before you start.

5. *The results of tests are not consistent with what I know about my child. What do I do?* Parents should report *specific behaviors* that they have noted that suggest inconsistencies with test scores. Perhaps your child did not concentrate on the day the test was given due to illness or some other reason and just "ticked off " answers. Or, because other subjects such as science and social studies become increasingly dependent upon reading in the sixth and seventh grades, your child may be affected by a slow reading rate. If the scores really do not agree with home observations, request that the child be retested.

6. *What happens to the score when you modify the test to meet the special needs of my child?* First, the test becomes a different test. Parents need to know how their child compares with *normal* children in order to set appropriate levels of expectation. If a test is modified to find areas of strength or weakness, the test may be so altered that it no longer compares your child and the normal population. What you have then is a special test for a special population. What it may tell you is how well this child can do this special task as compared to other special children, which is not always the information you need to know.

7. *I am concerned about my child's increasing difficulty. How can school records help me?* Note carefully how previous teachers have viewed your child since they offer important insights. Note carefully the negative comments: "disorganized," "untidy," "doesn't seem to be well disciplined," "doesn't ever finish work," "can't hold pencil"—which may be warning signs of learning difficulty. With the gifted child, school records may indicate that in the early grades the child mastered the material readily.

8. *Do classroom teachers receive the results of the special testing done with my child?* Not always! In many schools, records are stored in two places. Those that have to do with the child's attendance and academic performance are stored in the main office of the school, but those that record the results of special testing are stored in the office of special services. Although parents can see the results of both kinds of records, teachers may not have seen the information gained from diagnostic tests. Parents may want to convey to teachers the information they have learned, and request that teachers also be given the results from these tests that can help them with their teaching. *Ask* who gets copies of this testing!

9. *How do I know when progress is made?* When IEPs have been written for your child, these need to be evaluated on a yearly basis and children retested. Sometimes schools will use brief measures such as the *Wide Range Achievement Test* or the *Peabody Individual*

Achievement Test to evaluate progress. Parents need to be dubious of results indicating improvement from these brief tests, because if a child answers only a few questions more than at the beginning of the year, progress will be indicated. These brief tests are useful as screening tests, but inflate scores (and seeming progress) when used to evaluate a child's progress.

Parents should ask for evidence of progress from work records and the results of *broad-based achievement* tests and *mastery* tests.

10. *My child was given projective tests by the learning disabilities specialist and some problems were suggested. What do I do?* The learning disabilities specialist has not been trained to interpret emotional tests and should *NOT* make such diagnostic judgments. Parents need to insist that a properly trained person makes interpretation of personality tests and inventories of emotional adjustment. These tests do not necessarily serve as an indication for referral since children are likely to be inconsistent in their responses from one day to another when they are very young. Ask to have such findings reviewed with you by a psychologist. If a test indicates that your child is "anxious," use your common sense. Does your child behave in an anxious way? Does your child act fearful, scared of new experiences, report nightmares, have trouble sleeping, eating, act depressed or worried? Behavior is always a more reliable indicator of psychological health or sickness than inference from a projective test.

11. *Is my child's poor test performance due to anxiety during the testing?* The trained examiner works to establish a reassuring relationship with a child; praises the child for his or her efforts; and gives the child a great deal of individual attention. All these things help minimize the effects of anxiety on test performance. Most children say they enjoy the individualized testing sessions. If your child was ill on that day, be sure to report it and repeat the test.

12. *Can the SAT's (Scholastic Aptitude Tests) be given to learning disabled students under special conditions?* Yes. The special conditions allowed for learning disabled students include unlimited time, working in a room alone by oneself, use of a calculator, and if necessary, having a reader present. Such special conditions may give a distorted view of their future college performance. Students do not want to get into a college situation where they will be over their heads. Rather than electing the special conditions that are possible, many learning disabled students find that taking the SAT's twice is a better solution. It is also important that they take the *Preliminary Scholastic Aptitude Test* and use the study guides that are available. These latter procedures are used as well by students who are not learning disabled. Many students

take coaching sessions for these tests, which do increase scores. If your child does not have coaching, and others do, your child will be under a handicap.

13. *How should I prepare my child for special testing?* Parents should tell their child why they are being tested, and what will happen. Children with special needs are usually tested a lot, sometimes in conjunction with painful medical examinations, surgery, or medical tests. It becomes all the more important for parents to tell their child what kinds of tests they are likely to receive, when and where.

14. *How do children react to being told test results?* Many children respond well to being told what they can do well, and to being offered help in areas where they need it. But testing is also associated by many children with trouble. It is hard for most parents to hide their fears, disappointments, and concerns. Some children come away thinking that they haven't tried hard enough and that they cannot satisfy their parents. Parents can help their child by reacting realistically to test results, praising the good performances and planning immediate help—with their child—to improve the weaknesses.

15. *Is there a test for learning disability?* No. There is no one test used to diagnose learning disability. The judgment of learning disability is based on the results from several sources.

Parent participation and questioning is essential to working with children who have special needs. Parents need not be embarrassed to ask questions. They should ask about *anything* that is not clear. Many of the terms that are used are fuzzy, even for persons working in the field. You will not be jeopardizing your child's educational welfare to ask questions. Press for *clarity*. Be sure that you have received satisfactory answers to your questions. The ultimate goal of all involved is to set realistic expectations and plans. Parents need to keep questioning those confusing terms—"What is visual-perceptual impairment? What does it mean for my child?" "What does a deficit in sequential thinking mean? What can I do to help?" "What is spatial-temporal confusion?"

If you are confused, you are not alone! The field itself is confusing. Ask: "Why?" "What does it mean?" "How?" until you are satisfied that you understand. Some useful resources in this area are:

FARNHAM-DIGGORY, SYLVIA. *Learning Disabilities.* Cambridge, Massachusetts: Harvard University Press, 1978.

CLOSER LOOK, WASHINGTON, D.C. Free information regarding testing, programs, and the law for learning disabled and other children.

CHAPTER 11

Helping Your Child to Prepare for Tests and to Understand Test Results

Taking tests of one kind or another is part of every child's experience, both in school and out of school, as in these examples:

Tryouts for membership on a sports team
Tryouts for participation in the school band or drama production
Weekly checks on progress in school subjects, and during exam week

In fact, test-taking skill is one of the skills all of us need to acquire in order to deal successfully with our life experiences—taking a civil service test, taking a test to get a driver's license, or taking a licensing exam. As a continuous check of a child's learning, tests do matter. Children can be helped to take them.

Some children take tests easily and enjoy the challenge; others find the experience frightening. But, like learning to read, practice helps and most children can learn to take tests and become more at ease in the test-taking situation. Some of the ingredients for success in taking tests include

Wanting to do well	If success in learning is important to you, the parent, it is likely to be to your child also. The child's desire or motivation to succeed is important to doing well.
Confidence	Children gain confidence in themselves each time they are successful in an activity.

Preparation   In most cases, the child who re-
                               views for a test will do better on that
                               test than the child who puts off
                               studying.

Helping the Young Child to Take Tests

Paying attention and following directions are basic to taking tests
and, more generally, to success in school. The child who pays attention
and listens carefully will be better prepared to follow directions than the
child whose attention wanders and who then misses important details.
Note, for example, what might happen to the child who does not hear the
word "every" in the direction: "Mark every word that begins with the
letter b."

cat   boy   ball   house   bat

The child who marks only one word beginning with the letter b would
have followed only part of the direction.

For the young child, familiarity with the terms frequently used in
directions is also important. It might be that the young child does not
know the term "every" in the above direction and then would make a
mistake. The following words are among those used frequently in directions, particularly in the early grades, and need to be understood by the
child:

Words Frequently Used in Test Directions

start	every	missing	now
stop	all	matches	
	each		
over		first	
under	before	last	
	after		
on			
from	same	beginning	
to	different	end	

These words can be the basis of difficulty for the young child or the child
with special learning needs. The parent can help by providing experiences at home that incorporate the use of these terms. Some examples of
practices for parents will be included later in this chapter.

In addition to paying attention and following directions, it is important for the child to keep his or her place. Sometimes the young child is provided with a marker, other times not. In any case, the teacher needs to be constantly attentive to children who have visual or motor problems that might interfere with their keeping their place. The parent can help alert the teacher to these problem areas as well.

After the early grades, at about third or fourth grade, an answer sheet is introduced when tests are used throughout the school system. While answer sheets facilitate the enormous task of scoring tests and help reduce the school's expenses, they can also be the source of difficulty for some children. The child needs to be careful to keep his or her place and to avoid making stray marks on the answer sheet that might be counted as incorrect answers.

In summary, then, at least three general skills are required on the part of the child when taking tests in general, and one additional skill for taking systemwide tests.

All classroom tasks and tests require:

1. Paying attention
2. Following directions
3. Keeping one's place

Plus

Standardized tests and group tests with older children require:

1. Using an answer sheet

Helping the Child Develop Test-taking Skills

With the young child, readiness for following directions can be developed through the activities described below.

Playing Games

Games of all kinds can be both useful and fun for young children. Games can help the child learn to pay attention and concentrate, and the parent can praise the child's paying attention. Whether or not the child wins, his or her *efforts at trying* can be praised, which can help build confidence in trying.

Following Directions

Use important direction words (see page 127) in everyday home activities, when in the supermarket, or during family outings. The parent can use direction words when describing the position or placement of objects or retelling sequences of events such as "The box is on the bottom shelf " or "After we went to the store, we came home." It is also helpful to ask children to tell where objects are—"Where is the milk?"—and to describe events—"What happened when you first got to school today?"

The meaning of words and relationships can also be learned through making up games such as "What's missing?" or "Where is the _____ ?" or "Find one that matches."

Encouraging Questioning Behavior

Although the young child's many questions can sometimes be bothersome, the curiosity that underlies them helps children understand and gain information about their world. Some examples of encouraging responses that parents might wish to use include:

Smiles
Nods
Approving gestures
Hugs or pats on the back

Encouraging comments are also helpful such as "good," "excellent," "great," "that's right," "I'm really pleased with your good work," "good try," "good idea," "I like the way you did that," "much better," "look how many you did!"

Providing Varied Experiences

All the experiences that the child has are important. Parents, relatives, or friends can help by talking to the child about them—talking about items in the grocery store, things seen while riding the bus or in the car, household routines, and the child's play with other children.

Some children enjoy workbook and game books found in supermarkets and bookstores. If the child is interested in such activities, these books provide practice in activities such as keeping one's place on the page, connecting number dots that form pictures, looking for hidden pictures, and figuring out riddles. These activities are both motivating and fun, and also encourage thinking.

Helping the Older Child to Take Tests

We have already mentioned that most of the tests children take in the classroom provide teachers with an ongoing measure of their pupils' progress. Most children, particularly after the early grades, are likely to be faced with several such tests each week. How can a parent help a child prepare for these tests?

Find out what day of the week the usual classroom tests are likely to be given. In many elementary classrooms, for example, trial spelling tests are given on Wednesday and the final test on Friday. Thursdays and Fridays tend to be big days for other tests as well, such as in arithmetic or science. In junior high and high school, teachers usually indicate ahead of time when major tests are to be given. The schedule below is one example.

SAMPLE SCHEDULE OF ASSIGNMENTS AND TESTS

Week: *April 16 - 20*					
Assignments and Tests					
Subject (fill in)	Monday	Tuesday	Wednesday	Thursday	Friday
Mathematics	*pg 59, 1-25*	*pg 62, all*	*pg 65, even Q's*	*pg 68 all*	*TEST*
Science				*TEST on Unit 4*	
English	*Begin reading of Romeo & Juliet*		*In-class discussion*		*Quiz on Romeo & Juliet*
History	*Work on Project*				

Some teachers will also give surprise quizzes. Children usually figure out which teachers are likely to do this! Parents might wish to check that their child is maintaining a daily schedule, has prepared for the test, and does not stay up extremely late the night before the test.

The timing of standardized tests varies from one school system to another. A Calendar of School Testing (See Appendix A, p. 168) will give parents a general idea when these tests are likely to take place. Some school systems will inform parents when their children will be taking standardized tests, but if this does not take place, it is important for parents to ask.

A third area in which parents can help is with the child's actual preparation for the test. Practice does pay off! It is important to make sure that the child has reviewed important facts before taking a test. The following are some checkpoints to consider as your child prepares for tests.

Identifying What to Study

Pupils need to figure out the most important ideas covered and the most important terms to be learned. How should students go about this? Here are some pointers for your child:

1. Think about the things that have been emphasized in class, like notes the teacher wrote on the board, or material the teacher gave out.
2. In textbooks, the lead-in sentences to paragraphs, italicized words, and summary paragraphs generally include or are related to important information.
3. Think about the kinds of questions the teacher is likely to ask. Write them out and then answer them. The type of questions the teacher has asked before are a good place to start.
4. Plan a practice test which incorporates the above and test yourself.

Developing Study Skills

Study skills become increasingly important as the child progresses through the grades. Here are some suggestions about how to develop good study skills.

1. If students own their own textbooks, it is helpful to some children to underline important facts or ideas. When reviewing for a test, the underlined material will stand out.
2. If children summarize in their *own words* what they have read, right after they have read it, it helps them to remember.
3. Outlining material covered is helpful to some pupils.
4. When practicing a skill that needs to be memorized, the following procedure is helpful

   Do not try to memorize too much at one time—keep the unit to be memorized small.
   Practice the skill.
   Then spend time in another activity.
   Then review the skill.

5. Reword the material in your own words so you can answer different kinds of questions (what, when, where, why, and how).
6. In subjects such as science, social studies, and literature, the teacher is likely to ask "compare and contrast" kinds of questions in addition to factual questions. Pupils can anticipate some of these, such as: "What differences in climate affect how people in the north and south build houses? The kind of clothing they wear?" and so on. If your child seems to have trouble developing study skills, here are some study steps that your child might find helpful (see appendix G, If You Want More Information, for other reading related to study skills).

Steps For Effective Study

Organize your place of study.	1. Find a quiet place, and if possible shut off the TV and distracting music.
	2. Use this place of study regularly.
	3. Have present all materials you are likely to need—pencils, rulers, and so on.
	4. Have a dictionary present.
Organize your study time.	5. Study at a regular time each day.
	6. Take a short break between studying subjects; otherwise avoid interruptions (such as phone calls!).
	7. Reward yourself with a pleasing activity (phone call?) *after* you've completed your study, not before.
Organize your study activity.	8. Take notes about what is read, or outline it.
	9. Look up terms you don't know.
	10. Think through implications of what is read.
	11. Memorize important facts. Write them down and put the paper where you will see it often.
Preparing for tests.	12. Keep up with daily work to avoid cramming.
	13. Review notes, any material that has been read, and exercise pages.
	14. Restate what has been said, forming it into questions.
	15. Spend time on what you *do not* know.

Studying with a Friend

If your child has a friend to study with, studying together can really pay off—if they really study! This is particularly helpful at the junior high school level and above. Both pupils can think about what is most important and likely to be asked. They can quiz each other and gain extra practice.

A Pupil's Guide to Taking Tests

There are some important things to do when taking the test itself:

1. Read the directions carefully and think them through before beginning work.
2. Ask the teacher if you are not sure what the directions (not the questions) mean.
3. First, answer all the questions you know.
4. Be careful to keep your place! On special answer sheets make sure that you do not make any stray marks. Follow the instructions such as "Fill in the space above the letter that corresponds to the correct answer."

5. If there is a time limit, such as a class period, do not spend a lot of time on questions to which you *do not* know the answer. It is better to skip them at first. However, if you can narrow down the choices to one or two possibilities, it is generally useful to make your best guess. On some tests, particularly at the high school level and above, there can be a penalty for guessing. If this is the case, answer only the questions you know or can narrow down the choices to one or two. This is particularly true on many standardized tests and it is important to find out if a penalty for guessing will be imposed. If you can, try to pace yourself by dividing the amount of time allowed by the number of questions you need to answer.
6. If you have time, use it to check your answers. Some of the "silly" errors can be caught by checking. If you are not sure of the answer, *stick* with your *first* choice.
7. Try your best, that is what is most important.

Test Questions

The kinds of questions likely to appear on tests are:

Fill in the blanks (completion)	"There are _____ states in the United States."
True-False	"There are 12 things in a dozen." True _____ False _____
Multiple choice	"Who was the first president of the United States?" (a) Adams (b) Washington (c) Lincoln

Essay	"Compare the life of the early settlers before and after they came to America."
Short answer	"Give three reasons why it is important to eat a balanced diet."
Memory	"Write the months of the year."
Computation	"Multiply the following."

$$138 \qquad 382$$
$$\times 591 \qquad \times 921 \quad \dots$$

Problem solving	"List in order the steps you would take to solve the following problem. . . ."
Matching	"Match the following states and capitols:

Oregon   _____   1. Trenton
Connecticut _____   2. Salem
Tennessee   _____   3. Hartford
Wisconsin   _____   4. Springfield
New Jersey   _____   5. Madison
Illinois   _____   6. Nashville

Absences

If your child has been absent from school for any length of time, he or she may need some extra help to catch up on the work. Friday absences can put many children at a real disadvantage, since many classroom tests are given on Fridays.

Reacting to Your Child's Test Scores

There are rarely any problems when children score well. They will receive praise from their teachers, parents (do you?), and sometimes peers. The problem arises when a child has not scored well. The poor score may have occurred because the child did not study, because many careless errors were made, or because the child was not that skilled in that subject. Sometimes the poor score may have occurred because the child really did not know or understand the material being tested. In any case, the reaction of parents and teachers counts. Both can help the child by providing additional practice. Both can encourage the child's efforts to continue trying, rather than giving up when the material is hard. Both can help the child work out a better approach. A test score has nothing to do with the child's innate worth. But the reaction of the child's teachers and parents may influence the child's sense of self-worth and possibly the level

"some ways for you to make friends," or "see what kind of school program might be more interesting for you," or "how school can be a happier place for you," or "how you can learn best."

Some children know when they are encountering trouble and look forward to help with their problems, in fact are relieved when their parents have recognized this. Others resent the idea that they have a problem and do not want attention given to it. If the problem is one that needs help, and if you, as a parent have confidence in a particular specialist, then you have to be firm about the importance of going for an appointment. Most children prefer this to be done quietly, without announcing to the school and to all relatives that your child has an appointment with a psychologist or psychiatrist.

In each of the above examples, the person in charge is likely to meet with the parents after testing to describe the results. The parent can ask what to tell the child. Sometimes the child will be asked to participate during part of this meeting and will be told how he or she did. The opportunity to ask questions with the parents and examiner all present can help to clarify many problems or questions about interpretation.

Telling Your Child About His or Her Test Scores

During their years in school pupils will come to know very well the marks teachers give on weekly tests. The "A" in English, the 90 percent on the spelling test, the 4/50 on the science quiz are all scores with which children quickly become familiar. Sometimes however, particularly at the elementary school level, the results of the standardized tests of achievement that are given systemwide are not shared with pupils. Children may come home from school telling you that they took a big test, but not know how they performed. Children generally know those subjects that are hard for them or easy for them. But, since most standardized tests contain many questions which range from being simple to difficult, and may contain more questions than the child can answer during the time allotted, it is often difficult for children to know how they performed. The results of these tests may be given to parents at conference time or the results may be sent to parents through the mail. The parent coming home from a conference to the curious child may be unsure of what to say.

In our opinion it is very important that the child be told about his or her performance in a way that is helpful, as in the following examples.

You did very well in mathematics and received a score at the 60th percentile which is above average. You had more trouble in reading and scored at the 30th percentile in reading comprehension. Your teacher suggested that we try to find out why. I know that homework with a lot of reading is hard for you. In school the teacher will let you know when a reading specialist can come to do some special testing with you and help us find out what we can do.

or

Your scores in all areas were good and we're *very* pleased with your performance. You received an 83rd percentile in reading comprehension, 70th percentile in mathematics computation. . . .

Some publishers of standardized achievement tests have prepared special materials for pupils to explain their test results which the school may choose to use. One such example is the leaflet *How Are Your Basic Skills?* prepared by the publishers of the Iowa Tests of Basic Skills. This leaflet explains (1) the reasons for giving tests as an ongoing check on progress, (2) the skills that are tested, and (3) the meaning of scores on each skill area, using a chart of a sixth grade pupil to illustrate how to interpret areas of strength and those needing work, and finally (4) a chart of the individual pupil's scores.

Another example is the chart below for pupils taking the Stanford Intermediate Level I Achievement Tests.

	Number Right	Scaled Score	Grade Equiv.	%ile Rank*	STANINE*
TEST 1: Vocabulary					1 2 3 4 5 6 7 8 9
TEST 2: Reading Comprehension					1 2 3 4 5 6 7 8 9
TEST 3: Word Study Skills					1 2 3 4 5 6 7 8 9
TEST 4: Math. Concepts					1 2 3 4 5 6 7 8 9
TEST 5: Math. Computation					1 2 3 4 5 6 7 8 9
TEST 6: Math. Applications					1 2 3 4 5 6 7 8 9
TEST 7: Spelling					1 2 3 4 5 6 7 8 9
TEST 8: Language					1 2 3 4 5 6 7 8 9
TEST 9: Social Science					1 2 3 4 5 6 7 8 9
TEST 10: Science					1 2 3 4 5 6 7 8 9
TEST 11: Listening Comprehension					1 2 3 4 5 6 7 8 9
Total Battery (Test 1 through Test 11)					1 2 3 4 5 6 7 8 9
Total Auditory (Test 1 + Test 11)					1 2 3 4 5 6 7 8 9
Total Reading (Test 2 + Test 3)					1 2 3 4 5 6 7 8 9
Total Mathematics (Test 4 + Test 5 + Test 6)					1 2 3 4 5 6 7 8 9

*Percentile Ranks and Stanines based on tables for Beginning ☐ End ☐ of Grade

When discussing test results with the child it is important to:

1. Inform the child about areas of strength or those areas needing development.
2. Find out whether the child understands what the scores mean. For example, children frequently confuse the meaning of *percentile* with *percent correct*, thinking that the percentile score of 56 means he or she got only 56% correct (whereas it actually means that he or she scored at or above 56 percent of all children taking the test.

3. Avoid judgment as to the child's worth. The good scorer is no better—as a *person*—than the child receiving a low score.
4. Reassure the child who is having difficulty that you will try to find out the reasons why, and help.

Such a discussion can open the door for parents to have a useful interchange with their children about strengths and areas needing development. It can also be a time which allows the child to voice his or her opinion.

In summary, then, given the age and needs of the child, the child should be informed in as constructive a way as possible about the results of testing *and* the steps to be taken to help solve any problems.

CHAPTER 12

Selecting a School for Your Child

Evaluating Public School Systems

What do you do when you move to a new part of the country and want to find a good public school for your child? If you talk to real estate brokers, they may tell you that a house bought in this community, or in this location, has a very good school. How do you *know* if it is a good school? There are several steps you can take that will help you find out whether it is a good school, depending on what you consider "good."

Step 1: Using Census Information

The first thing you should do is to familiarize yourself with the community itself, because it is the community that supports the school in terms of policy and taxes. The taxpayers of the town set the agenda for the school. The most accurate information about a community will be found in census tract data. Call the nearest office of the Census Bureau (part of the U.S. Department of Commerce) and ask where you can find census tract data for the communities you are interested in. Not all communities have these data, but all the large cities do, and many of the large suburbs. A small country town will not.

Let us assume that you are moving to Big City and you have decided to locate near that city. You have commuting to consider, so you probably have a limited choice of communities. One consideration is going to be the cost of housing which is one index of a community's affluence. Find the most recent census tract data for the communities in which you are interested. If necessary, ask someone from the Census Bureau or a nearby university library to help you locate the correct tables.

You want to look for three things. The first is *income,* which is usually expressed as "median family income." That means the family income at the midpoint. Half of all families' total income will be below and half will be above. Median is used in the sense of a median divider which divides a road exactly in half. Look at the median family income for the communities you are interested in. You will see a difference in the amount of money that the median family earns. You might be wise to try to pick a community whose income is close to your own, so that you will not be the richest, or the poorest, in that community. Be sure to check how recently the census tract data were collected and make adjustments for inflation. In 1970 the median family income across the country was $9590, which was quite a few years ago and does not reflect changes in the economy since then. At this writing, median family income is around $15,000 a year.

The next thing to look at is *education* which is expressed in "number of years completed." A high school education is expressed as 12 years. An eighth grade education is 8 years. Above 12 years represents the number of years of higher education, such as college, graduate training, and professional training. If your family is well educated, then probably you will want to be in a community where other people are also highly educated, because you will share similar interests and support the same policies at the school. If, for example, the adults in your family average the completion of college, which would be 16 median school years completed, then you would look for a community which is more like you, which probably has a median year of 13.5. Although 13.5 is not the same as 16, you must remember that this average takes into account *all* adults in a community, of which many who are older did not attend college. You might not be so happy in a community where the median years completed of education was 9.2, which represents a sizable difference. In 1970 the median years completed across the country as a whole was 12.1; 52 percent of our population completed high school. These figures provide benchmarks for comparison. If education is a very important value in your family, and you are an educated family, then you want to lean toward the community which has the highest median years completed in education and the highest percentage of those completing high school, only because you are going to find yourself in a community of like-minded people when it comes to schooling.

The third factor is the *occupational* breakdown provided in the tables of the census tract data. The census usually presents this information by seven categories starting with the professional, followed by managerial, clerical, sales, then service workers, and so on. These categories are very broad and sometimes can be misleading. In a heavily industrialized portion of a city, obviously one will find many machine operatives and craftsmen. In a white collar suburb one would find a higher percentage of managerial and professional. Compare the communities you are interested in by these characteristics and decide what is the best occupational mix for your particular family. Obviously the higher the occupational mix, the more likely it is that the income level will be up, as well as the number of years of education. One might think that the best community would be the one that is highest in income, education, and occupation, but that is not necessarily so. You might find that your family did not fit into such a community, or would have trouble keeping up with the Joneses, which can put terrible financial stress on a family. It is probably wiser to pick a community where you will be about in the middle financially, educationally, and occupationally.

If you are a minority family, you will want to look carefully at the race breakdown. Perhaps you want a community where there is a national average of 11 percent black, or perhaps you want a community where the percentage is higher. If you are a Spanish-speaking family, you will have trouble with census information because Spanish speaking is considered an ethnic breakdown, not a racial category, and therefore is not reported in census data.

By the time you finish inspecting the census tract data for the communities you hope to be choosing, you will know a good deal about your area before you even go into it. It is amazing what some apparently dull tables can tell you about a community, particularly if you compare it to others! You can almost predict what the school will be like. For example, let us look at the occupational breakdown. The best *single* bet anyone can make about the future occupations of the children in a school system is that they will follow the occupations currently pursued by their parents. (Often they do not, and it is true that many young people today do not want to follow their parents' occupation, but the statement still holds true that it is the best *single* bet.) If a high proportion of adults in school system A is professional and managerial, it is very likely that the children in that school are going to be oriented toward going to college and further training, and will take up those same occupations. In school B where a high proportion of parents are employed in manufacturing or agricultural occupations, the best bet you can make is that the students in that school will elect those kinds of jobs.

Step 2: Reading Newpaper Files

The next bit of research that will pay off for you is to go to the local newspaper office. Ask to see their files for the past two or three years. Ask when the board of education generally meets and then look at the papers for the following day, if it is a daily. By reading about what has been happening at the local board of education, you will learn what the issues have been. Newspaper stories will tell you about mil rates, about tax bases, about issues over books, and courses, and most of all, about the budget. A school budget tells you what school policy is. It tells you how much the school tax is compared to other communities, something you definitely want to know about if you are buying a home. The budget, in terms of what is cut out of it, tells you what the school will *not* support. From reading the newspaper file, and talking to the education editor if you possibly can, you will learn whether the taxes are going up or going down, and how the mil rate compares to the actual value of real estate. A mil rate means the tax per $1000 of appraised property. Mil is an abbreviation for "mille" which is Latin for 1000. Communities in the past have varied a good deal in their methods of appraising property. A house that would sell on the open market at $50,000 may be appraised at 50 percent of its value, which would be $25,000. The school tax then might be based on a certain mil rate for the $25,000, its appraised value as opposed to its fair market value. One needs to know not only the mil rate, but what *percentage* of the fair market value is set in that community. There is a tendency now to have communties set their appraisal values at fair market value, meaning what you could actually get for your property on the open market.

In reading the files of the newspaper or talking to the education editor, be alert to the shift in population. In some communities the size of the population has been decreasing in the last few years. You may be moving into a community where there has been no new industrial growth, so that numbers of children coming to school may have decreased. This may mean a closing of neighborhood schools. What about the school for your future neighborhood?

When you read the newspaper files, it is a good idea to check the editorial page occasionally to see what the newspaper's policy has been toward the board of education. You may find out that there has been a terrific struggle over a superintendent and his policies that will give you a lot of insight into community feeling. You also want to know how often the school budget has been passed in recent years; what the conflict has been; over what issues; and by what community groups. It is very common for a taxpayers' group or some other economy-minded group to attack the school budget, particularly teachers' salaries, as being wasteful. This argument is carried in the paper which reports what happens at the open meetings of the board of education. It is wise to follow these accounts because it will give you a good insight into the different groups in the community and how the community as a whole stands on cutting the school budget. Did the teachers get a raise last time around? Was there a long and bitter teacher's strike (which is usually a very detrimental factor in terms of faculty morale)? Have the schools been closed for any period of time due to budgetary struggles? Have the schools decided to close in the winter to save fuel bills? If so, and if this is a family of working parents, then you must think about what you will do for the children during the two to three weeks in the winter when the schools are closed. What platforms have the board of education members run on? Generally you will find some economy-minded candidates, some conservative candidates, and some curriculum enrichment candidates running for these offices.

Now let us suppose you have done your homework, having looked at the census tract data (step one) and run down to the newspaper to see the files and to talk with the reporter who covers the board of education (step two). You now have a good deal of information about the various communities into which you plan to move. What can you predict? If the census tract data tell you this is a high income, high education, high occupation community (these factors make up "SES" or "socio-economic status"), then you can be reasonably sure that the schools will put a good deal of emphasis on college after high school—and therefore on achievement; and therefore on test scores; advanced placement; honors classes; and the ability of the school to get its graduates into the more prestigious colleges. At the other end of the SES scale, if the community is less affluent, less educated, and in lower occupational jobs, the school will more likely be concerned with the availability of jobs after high school; with trade schools that prepare their graduates for actual job openings; with discipline; and with a budget where teachers do not make a salary that is considered higher for nine months than what the hard-working parents of the community earn in twelve months.

Step 3: Determining the Achievement Level

The first thing an educational psychologist wants to know about a school is its achievement level, and the same thing should be true for parents. However many reservations we may have about achievement tests and about too much emphasis sometimes on achievement, the fact remains that how fast students learn in a particular school is absolutely *critical* to your child's progress and happiness in that school. If your child is an average child, meaning that he learns at an average rate, and he transfers into a school that is very quick moving, with children who are very quick learners, he will be at the back of the pack and be miserable, quite naturally. You want to make a good *match* between your child's learning rate and that of the school. The easiest way to do this, and it is very important that you do so, is to look at your child's achievement test results over the past few years. With the help of this book you should be able to figure out where your child stands in terms of national percentiles. Is your child the kind that tests around the national average percentile or grade equivalent? Is he or she about at or around the 50th percentile on most tests? Is he or she at the 75th or the 25th? Where does your child stand? Then compare that number with the school's achievement to see if you are making a good match.

For example, let us say your daughter is a lovely child but just not a scholar. Her scores on most of the tests range between the 35th and the 40th, maybe sometimes the 45th percentile on most tests. She is now in fifth grade and you have had to move. You have a choice of two schools in front of you. In west neighborhood that you might live in, the west school she would go to contains children who average six months ahead of the national average, using grade equivalent scores. That means that when they are in the middle of fifth grade, they will be handling subject matter that comes at the end of fifth grade. This puts them above the 50th percentile. What would happen to your lovely daughter in that kind of school? She is not going to feel very lovely when she finds out that no matter how hard she works, she cannot catch up with the rest of the class or the rest of the school.

On the other hand you have a choice of putting her in east school which, everything else being equal (which it never is), is running a little bit below the national average. When the school was tested, in the fifth grade fifth month the children averaged about fifth grade third month on reading and other subject matter. In terms of achievement this might be a better school for your daughter because she would be near the middle of the learning rate of the other pupils, which gives her a chance to succeed.

There are other things to take into account, of course. You will not buy a house in the area of east school just because of achievement. But it should be a very big red flag to parents not to put a child into a school where everyone else is going to learn much faster than their child. It is unfair to the child. It will make even the nicest, happiest, merriest child into a discouraged person. No one likes to be behind all the time and behind all the other people.

Step 4: Evaluating the Grading System

You may be surprised to learn that you want to know how the pupils are graded. Why is this so important? In general (and of course there are exceptions) the more specific the grading system, and the earlier it is put into practice, the more academically oriented the school is likely to be. School A is a school where parents get paragraph reports from the teacher through sixth grade. The grades given are "S" for satisfactory, sometimes with a plus or minus, "O" for outstanding, and "U" for unsatisfactory. If this practice is held to through the sixth grade, it is very likely to be a school that is not as scholastically oriented as one in which letter grades are given beginning as early as first or second grade, accompanied by teacher descriptions; or a system whereby numbers are given such as 73, 82, 91, and so on. When you stop to think about it, this makes a certain amount of sense. The more a school is interested in scholastic achievement, the more attention it will pay to the way achievement is measured.

The measures used can range from soft, gurgly adjectives that don't tell very much to a parent, to the perhaps overly refined 83 as compared to an 84 for a semester's work. The grading system your child enters is *very* important, as important as the salary system in a corporation. The grading system is how your child is going to be evaluated, and the means whereby you will be informed of your child's progress. Go over to the school, and ask to see a sample of the report cards from grade 1 on up, asking for a copy of the report each time it changes. A common time for a report card to change is around third grade, and around sixth grade. By junior high school at the latest the norm is to mark pupils in grades from A to F. It can be a very rude shock for a child who has been graded as "S" throughout six years of schooling to walk into junior high school then receive a C or a D. To that child "satisfactory" means he is doing all right, but to the teacher "satisfactory" meant about a C level of work.

Step 5: Learning About the Testing Program

The next thing you want to find out about is the testing program. Why do you want to know so much about the testing program? Because (1) the testing program is going to be the basis for evaluating your child and (2) it tells you something about the philosophy of the school. If one school system you look at does no testing with standardized tests except at first grade and seventh grade, you might be a little uneasy because you are going to spend six years wondering how your youngster does on standardized tests. During that time he may be getting excellent marks from teachers who find him very attractive and pleasant. This is not the same as knowing how he stacks up on a nationally standardized test. On the other hand, schools can go overboard with testing, although during times of strict budgets it is not very likely. You may want a school system that tests every other year so that you have some good information coming in every two years about how your youngster is doing, apart from what the teacher evaluations tell you. Ask (politely!) how the test scores are reported to the parents and to the pupils. If a form is used to report results, ask to see a copy so that you know the kind of information you are going to be getting. If the school office tells you that these scores are not reported to parents, you may have a strong reservation about how much information will be made available to you. It does not sound like a school system that wants to share very much information with parents.

Step 6: Examining the Curriculum

Now let us look at the curriculum, a subject we have not even mentioned so far, which may seem odd. Let us look at the options. Ask a guidance counselor to tell you (so you can write it down) all the optional courses in the high school. There will probably be quite a few of them. In one school the counselor tells you that your child, if he or she is so inclined, and sufficiently able, could elect courses in advanced Russian, Renaissance art, advanced photography, and music theory. This is one kind of school. In another school, the school counselor tells you that the options are typing, home economics, mechanical drawing, drafting, and "vo-ag" (vocational agriculture). That is a different school. One is not necessarily better than the other; they are very different. The question is: which one is going to suit your child better? Today many optional courses are given in response to student interest, so a list of optional courses will tell you the interests of students in that school. You might want to fit that interest pattern with that of your child.

Step 7: Checking the School Schedule

The next thing to look at may seem like an unusual suggestion. Go look at the school schedule. Ask a guidance counselor to give you a copy of a typical schedule for someone in the grade that your child would be entering. Ask for two or three different schedules so that you can get some idea of the range. If you can, try to get a copy of the master schedule. The way a school spends its time tells you what its priorities are. You want to pay particular attention to the number of study halls that students average in the high school. Some students seem to major in study halls, having as many as 2 to 3 a day, back to back—a waste of time because very little studying goes on in most such halls. In some other schools, the schedule is backbreaking. A youngster will go from one course to another course all day, without any break, and also be expected to carry five heavy subjects, and sometimes six. This is a heavy load for any child.

If your child has special interests, and most do, be sure to check them out. Is there a swim team? What about band? What about music instruction? What about art? What about soccer or ballet or a chess club or a cooking club or a nature club? Get a list of the clubs as well as the optional courses so that you have some picture of what the educational menu is. Be sure to check who is eligible. Often schools will tell you that all these optional courses are available in their schools. But when you get down to the nitty gritty, you may find that only blue-eyed tenth graders who have a free period at 10:00 on Wednesday can actually get into the chess club.

Step 8: Examining the Budget

Look at the school budget, which is not great fun to do, but the budget reflects the priorities. What the community supports in money is what it considers important. You certainly want to look at teachers' salaries in comparison to salaries in the neighboring communities. It is an old axiom, but true, that teachers tend to gravitate to those school districts where they are paid better. The school district with higher salaries becomes attractive, it can select teachers from a wider pool, and the chances are that you will end up with higher quality teaching. (The same thing seems to happen in the rest of the working world!)

How much is being spent on athletic activities? If your child is a girl, is the athletic budget earmarked for all the male activities, such as football, or will your daughter get a fair share of the sports equipment and training in whatever activity she enjoys? You notice there is money in the budget for refitting the science lab. That suggests that this school cares about its science program. Another school might spend money on a fitness room. That shows different priorities. What does the superintendent say about the frills that can be cut out of the budget, if a cut is necessary? How educators define a frill shows you a good deal about their educational philosophy. ("His" is used advisedly here because there are only a handful of women school superintendents.) When budgets have to be cut, one community will do anything, including having bake sales, to keep its basketball team; another will do the same for its band; and another will fight for library acquisitions. These are three different kinds of schools.

Step 9: Visiting the School

There is absolutely no substitute for walking the halls of the school in which you are interested. There is a great deal to be seen, but one has to do it with a few antennae out. An experienced school person can walk the halls of a school for 10 or 15 minutes and come back and tell you almost to the "t" that school's priorities. An inexperienced visitor can walk for 10 or 15 minutes but only notice that the school seems pleasant, and that the children's drawings that were on the bulletin board looked very attractive. What does one look for in the halls of a school?

Every school has its own culture. What it posts in its halls to show to its visitors and other members of the school staff speaks a great deal about what the school views as important. How pupils and teachers move through the halls tells us a great deal, as well as the appearance of the students and faculty. How are the students dressed? Are they in fancy blue jeans or in uniform? Are they dressed according to some kind of school dress code? Are they dressed expensively or modestly? Do the boys wear shirts and ties, or tee shirts? Do they come to school in the latest or trendiest and most expensive outdoor boots or in old sneakers? Observing how children dress in a school tells you a good deal about the level of income in the community as well as the amount of attention—or inattention—the school gives to the appearance of its pupils. To some parents it is important that children dress at a certain level to attend school, and to other parents it is a matter of no importance. The degree to which standards are relaxed about dress probably is an indication that the school does not think appearances are very important. The more informal the dress, probably the more informal you will find the school as a whole.

Faculty dress will tell you something as well. Do the women teachers wear skirts or do they wear slacks? Are the men dressed informally or formally? The more informal the faculty dress, the more likely that children and faculty are on a first name basis, and that the school conducts its adult to child relationships in an informal manner. There are exceptions, of course, but on the whole this seems to be true.

Visit a few classrooms, even if only for a minute. If you cannot get into the classrooms, linger by the door which you hope contains a glass panel, and look in. A very quick survey will tell you something about the degree of orderliness in the school. It is not true that a child can only learn sitting at a desk with feet on the floor. A child can read with great enjoyment curled up in a corner. But there is a *difference* between purposive informality and chaos. In a school in East Africa, when a visitor walks in, all children rise and in chorus say "good morning" to the visitor. That is one level of orderliness. At the other extreme are classrooms where a stranger can walk in and out, entirely unnoticed by the children, hopefully because they are so engrossed in the work at hand, but sometimes because the din and confusion in the room obscure the visitor. Orderliness is important in the classroom, not so that we can make automatons of the children, but only because without some order and quiet there can be no learning. In order for instruction to take place, children have to be able to hear their teacher and hopefully to pay attention to the teacher so that they can be instructed. If the classrooms are running at 110 decibels, it is very unlikely that instruction is taking place.

Try to walk through the cafeteria during lunch hour, and through the gym if your guide will let you. In some cafeterias, the amount of disruption and food waste that occur are unbelievable. In some, students throw food at each other, or see if it will stick on the ceiling. This may be important to you! Take a look at the menu or the steam table and see what is being served. Depending upon your interest in nutrition, the school may be appealing to you or not. Walk down the corridors between classes. The time between classes, perhaps 2 minutes, sometimes 5 minutes, is a terribly important social time for students in any school. This is when they give messages to each other and have a quick conversation. It is the marketplace of the school as far as the children are concerned. See how the school handles it. Do the teachers line up outside the classrooms and reprimand the children for being noisy? Does it look like an army drill? Do the kids move quietly from room to room? Do they ever stop to talk to a teacher in a friendly way, or are all interactions impersonal? Do you see a teacher talking to a youngster in an interested way after the bell rings? If you are visiting a public high school, walk through the parking lot and look at the kinds of cars out there. That will tell you a good deal about the economic level of the school.

Be sure to walk through the front door for visitors at some point. Possibly you have been wandering around on your own, but be sure to go in that front door and see how visitors are handled. The front office is as much a way of announcing the school as any publication that the school puts out. In some schools, you walk in the front door to be met with a sign that reads "All visitors must register in the principal's office." That announces one kind of school, clearly one that does not trust visitors. In another school one is invited in with a friendly sign and the office staff actually notices you. Look at the walls between the front door and the office to see what is displayed. Sports trophies? Academic honor roll? An exhibit of current art work? Posters for a play? Cheerleading activity for an upcoming game? What is posted in those front halls is the way a school announces itself by saying "this is the kind of school we are."

And then to the office itself. This is the nerve center of the school from an administrative point of view. (From the students' point of view the important places are the corridors, the lockers, the cafeteria, the gym, and the bathrooms, plus the area outside the school where students congregate before and after.) Some school offices are as bureaucratic, impersonal, and as rude as those to be found in some government agencies. No one looks up from the typewriter when you walk in; no one notices you until you faint, cough, or drop something. In other offices, even of the same size, the receptionist will greet you with a smile and make you feel welcome, offer you a magazine of recent vintage and chat about the weather while you wait to see the principal or assistant principal. Most will offer you a cup of coffee that is guaranteed to be a solvent for anyone's stomach liner.

Look around the office. What is posted in it? Is it an office that says through its notices, "O.K. everybody get your work done because I am watching?" Are there notices to the faculty to get their book lists in? How are these reminders phrased? Are they funny or are they arbitrary sounding? Are there cartoons that have been cut out and hung up recently? Then take a look at the way the office is organized. The location of the different offices tells you a lot about the school. If you walk into a school office which has the assistant principal or vice-principal's office next to it, with a long row of hard chairs just outside the door, you know that you are in a school where discipline is considered a major function of the office. If guidance counselors' offices are located nearby with lots of college material, that gives quite a different appearance to the front office. How are students greeted in the office? Are they welcomed and referred to by name? Or are they treated as intruders? How do students act in the office? Do they act as if their lives are being threatened, or do they act as if it is a pleasant place to come? It is a wise idea to come fifteen minutes *ahead* of time for any appointment you might have in the school office, so that you can pick up the school culture by walking slowly through the halls on your way to the front office, getting lost a few times, and then having a little extra time in that front office to look around you.

After you have done all of the above, it is *now* time to read the official information about the school's policies, goals, objectives, and so on, all of which are helpful, but they tend to be official pronouncements·as opposed to the steps we have outlined here which tell you what the school is really about.

The most important person in a school is its chief administrator, who is usually the principal. This is the person that sets the tone of the school. This is the person who models behavior for the rest of the staff, either good or bad. By all means, try to meet with the principal. If not, see the principal in operation at a public meeting, or at a board of education meeting, or at a talk before the students. Getting some sense of what the principal is like will help you to understand what the school is like.

In independent schools the principal is called the headmaster or headmistress ("head"). They are even more important in the independent schools than they are in public schools because there is more leeway in an independent school as to the goals it might choose.

Choosing an Independent or Private School: Coed, Boarding, or Day

Be sure to reread the previous step nine about visiting a public school (pages 148 to 151) before you go to a private school, because most of the same things apply.

A word first about school facilities. Facilities do *not* make an education. Good education can take place in a dank cellar if the teacher is gifted and the students are motivated. Perhaps Americans tend to emphasize facilities more than other people because we are such an affluent nation. Do not be taken in by gorgeous classrooms, computer labs, one-way vision mirrors, gyms, pools, playing fields, ice rinks, and indoor tennis courts. It certainly speaks of the affluence of the school, but it does not tell you about the quality of the education. It is likely that a wealthy school can afford to attract better teachers, but it is not necessarily so. Sometimes faculty are attracted to schools of that kind because it gives them a good income and a pleasant life with many perquisites. But wealthy schools do not necessarily attract those people who are intellectually devoted to teaching, which is the most important facility. Not all good teachers are willing to live out their adult life in a green and brick park populated by teenagers. Private boarding schools attract a certain number of faculty who have an income of their own, who themselves are graduates of private schools, who like the country life and cross-country skiing, but who are not intellectual giants.

There are also faculty in these schools who are among the very best teachers you or your child are ever going to see, who willingly devote themselves to instructing the young in the beauties of Chaucer and the significance of German history. If there were some guaranteed way to determine where the great teachers are, then this chapter need not have been written. Probably your child is going to be influenced by teachers at this high school age and in a boarding school environment, more than by *any* other teaching experience in his or her life. Your child will be in daily contact with teachers who, if they are conscientious, are going to be totally on top of what your child produces. There will be smaller classes, and more individual attention. It is here that your child can learn standards of work, how to think rationally, and what it feels like to have the mind stretched. It can be an enormously important experience, if the quality of teaching is there.

Every private school has its own history and reputation. Its reputation is harder to identify than its history, so start with its history. Most boys' boarding schools were established in a religious tradition if they are located in the Middle Atlantic and New England areas. Perhaps that religious tradition does not show today, but it is an important part of the school's culture. Many of these schools were established originally by ministers of a Protestant denomination to school the sons of neighboring families who desired a classical education superior to that available in the local public schools. Read the catalog for history. Look to see how recently the head has been a minister. If religious education is a significant aspect of school life for you—either positive or negative—check to see if chapel is required, and how often. Is a course in religious education required of all seniors, for example?

Every school has its own culture, usually set by the head. Part of what you are selecting in a school is a set of values. Nothing, except the quality of teaching, is as important as that set of values. If the school has a long religious tradition, you may be comfortable with a value system that puts character high on its list. Another school may have left its religious roots long ago, and its value system may be getting ahead, achievement, or high grades. Search out the value system as carefully as you can, because it is the culture your child will be living in for the next three or four years.

How do you identify a school's values? One way is to read carefully about its trustees. What do they do for a living? Are all bankers and all male? That would suggest a financial set of values, at least at first blush. A mixture of lawyers and bankers (not uncommon)? Where do they work? Where were they educated? Are they all alumni of the school, which would suggest a rather narrow band of experience for a board of trustees? Are there any educators on the board? How accomplished are the trustees in their own right, as opposed to status based on inherited position and wealth? If a girls' school, is its board of trustees composed of women (and men) who are accomplished in their own right, or who have status based upon marriage? The board of trustees usually represents the values of the school. Perhaps even more important, the board, unless it has relinquished its power to a strong head, will have considerable influence on what the school does. If the head proposes new programs, such as a new dormitory, a new gym, a new science lab, and a new computer, *which* will the board support, and raise the money for? Given the board of trustees of the schools in which you are interested, can you predict which program they would support?

If it is possible, try to find a way to meet one or two members of the board of the schools in which you are particularly interested. Ask them about the history of the school; what do they see as its unique character, compared to other schools in its class; and if they are graduates, what about their education at this school was especially meaningful to them?

Schools change, often radically, occasionally drastically. What has been a top school suffers from one or two poor heads; the better faculty move; the quality of students declines; endowment drops off; and the school gets a reputation for being in trouble. When a school gets this reputation, experienced advisers in the private day schools will try to steer a student and the student's family away from the school. Listen carefully to the advice you receive from the school advisers in your child's day school. If your child is in public school, seek out an interview (and make a contribution to the school) with a school adviser in the best private school nearby. There is an inner circle of information among private (read "independent") schools. They know which head has left, or is rumored to be leaving, and this is a crucial piece of information. The head is the model in private school—who sets the educational priorities, upholds selected values, and gives the board of trustees certain choices of programs to support. If a head is about to leave or retire, and the new head has not been chosen, be careful. Try to find a school where you know who will be in charge for the next 3–4 years. A well-informed school adviser in an independent school can also help you match the right level of academic toughness with your child's ability. Boarding schools have their own academic pecking order. It is generally known that school M is very competitive, and that school G is for children with learning problems. There may be very good reasons for choosing school G if your child needs the resources and the slower pace of that school, but would be miserably behind in fast-moving school M.

Not only do schools change, but schools go in and out of favor with students. This year everyone wants to go to school P, which is coed. Last year school S was in for boys, and school Q for girls. These fads may not be based on anything more than superficial characteristics, but in the independent school world, your child may feel strongly about going to a school that is "in" this year.

So, before you visit the school, do your homework. Read the catalogs, not just this year's, but a few years back to see what has been consistently emphasized. Check on the heads and how long they have lasted. Lots of turnover in heads is a poor sign, for it may signal a lack of definition in the school's values, a volatile board, money troubles, or a governance structure that a head cannot tolerate. Read the faculty list carefully. Where were they educated? How advanced are their degrees? How long have they been teaching there? Look for a stable faculty, with varying lengths of service but certainly a good proportion who have been there 15 or more years. The younger the faculty, the more education is to be expected. Years ago, many fine teachers received a bachelor's or a master's degree, and were well educated. Today, a doctorate is not uncommon, or two master's degrees. Note how many of the teachers are graduates of the school. If the proportion is high, one would worry about inbreeding. A school that can attract a faculty from diverse universities, and not graduates of their own school, is often a school that is attractive to faculty. A school that is attractive to faculty often is a school that cares about teaching and the life of the mind.

Are faculty wives also employed as faculty, full or part-time? This is an old practice about which there are two sides. Some faculty wives are very well educated and very able teachers, employable quite in their own right, but because they are located on an isolated school campus, they often do not have other employment opportunities. Some wives are hired for matters of convenience, to add income to a faculty family, or to fill in, quite inexpensively, for a vacant post. How can you tell the difference? Examine the academic credentials. Have they been promoted over the years? How responsible is their position?

Read about last year's class, and the year before, and the year before. What colleges did they enter? This is the *crucial* test of an independent school. What colleges their graduates enter tells us the school's academic standing, in a very competitive college race.

Read about the curriculum. What courses are required? What is the range of electives? Do they fit your youngster's interests?

Familiarize yourself with the school's history. Talk to as many graduates as you can. Call the alumni office and ask for names of graduates in your area. Many schools have an alumni (or alumnae) council that screens applicants in each large community, so feel free to talk to that graduate and ask as much as you can. Remember that the alumnus/alumna is also looking you over as a prospective parent, so take pains with your questions so that they are phrased in a nonantagonistic manner.

By doing your homework before you visit, you will be much better prepared to learn more while you visit.

We would suggest when you visit the school that you ask to sit in on some classes, which means visiting on a regular school day. Take the time! Sit in on as many as you possibly can, to get some idea of the quality of teaching. There is no one way to teach, and there is no one style of teaching that is superior. But certainly you can pick up the intellectual quality of the classroom by sitting in a few classes. Listen to the quality of the questions the teacher asks. See how quickly the discussion moves along. How much are the students being challenged? Does the teacher respect their opinions? Does a teacher follow up on a piece of illogic? Is the class period well planned and organized? Is there an air of intellectual excitement among the students?

Get a copy of the school schedule, just as you would do in a public school. Ask for a typical schedule, or ask to see several, so that you know exactly how the students spend their time. This shows the real priorities of the school. Look at the number of class minutes and the number of classes in each subject per week. If your child is going to be getting French just twice a week for 40 minutes each, there is a very good chance he or she will be learning very little French. It is very hard to learn a language in 80 minutes a week of class time. To what extent are nonmajor subjects an important part of the schedule? How many subjects do most students take?

Compare the endowment of this school with that of other schools you are interested in, and compare their financial aid. If you are hoping for help financially for your child's education, this is going to be crucial. The amount of endowment also tells you a good deal about the school's options. Some private boys' boarding schools are very wealthy. They can afford to build all kinds of facilities, and can pay a faculty member well, which means they can choose from a larger faculty pool.

What provision is made for a child who is having trouble in a subject? Most schools will tell you that teachers are available for after school help, during study halls, or by appointment. Sometimes this is more lip service than reality. Ask specific questions: "How often are students seen by teachers?" "For how long for extra help?" "Is there anybody on the faculty whose specific responsibility it is to help children who have educational problems?" "Are there any computer programs available to help a child struggling with a difficult mathematics unit?" "Is there a reading teacher available for those who need to step up their speed of reading or who have some trouble with it?"

Some Special Considerations for Your Daughter

It has been the fashion recently for boys' schools to go coed by admitting girls, or by joining with a nearby girls' school. It is rare to go the other way, although Vassar College has gone coed by admitting male students. If your daughter wants to attend a coed school, it is important for you to find out how interested that school is in a girl's education by taking several steps. (1) You first want to know what percentage of the school is girls, as opposed to boys. Then you want to see how many women faculty members hold appointments as faculty members (rather than as wives of teaching husbands), because you are looking to see if the school contains role models for your daughter. An interesting anecdote about the importance of role models is that Radcliffe College attracted some of the very brightest girls as students, but as graduates they were not achieving at the level their academic promise would have suggested. One interpretation of this has been that these bright girls were educated in an environment where they had no female role models. All they ever saw were male Harvard professors. Girls *need* role models if you want them to become achieving women. They need women who are on the faculty in their own right, as achieving persons. If, on the other hand, your goal for your daughter is not an achieving one, then you will be content for her to be at a school where all the role models are male, where she is very likely to take up the role of handmaiden.

You will want to check to see what facilities are available for girls. Will she have the same access as the boys to the sports facilities? Can she work in the photography room the same amount of time as the boys? On the computer? In the science lab? How many girls are there in the advanced courses in mathematics and science? One parent says that this has been a problem for her daughter in a boys' school, recently turned coed— because there are no girls in these advanced courses. If a girl is talented in either science or mathematics, it puts a high price on her courage to be the *only* girl in a class of all boys taking an advanced subject.

Is someone on the faculty specifically responsible for being helpful to girls? What are the dormitory facilities? Are there female dormitory parents available? In choosing a coed school for your daughter, as opposed to your son, you need to be aware that girls may be considered second-class citizens in a boys' school, not just because of traditional sexist attitudes, but because of girls' records as alumnae donors. Women in the past have not been very financially supportive of their own schools, and consequently have not been considered a very good bet financially for a school. This influences a school's admissions decisions, quite naturally, since accepting a student is also accepting (hopefully) a future alumnus or alumna.

These are some of the steps you can take either before your visit or investigate while you are making the visit. There are some things you can inquire about during the visit itself that will help. Students are often assigned by the admissions office to be on duty to take visitors around. Obviously, the school picks student escorts who are considered good representatives of the school. You are probably not seeing a typical student when you are being escorted. You are seeing a better than average student in terms of appearance, academics, and manners. Be sure to make many reinforcing and complimentary comments about the school and about your guide during your visit. Such remarks create pleasant conversation (even if you instantly dislike the school and plan never to return); in addition, you will learn much more from a guide to whom you have been complimentary than one you have treated abruptly. If you are interested in the school, you should realize that you are under observation also, and that your escort will report something about what you are like . . . so be on your good behavior. Your guide will probably try to find out what your child's interests are. A typical pattern is for a guide to find out what your child is interested in and then make an especially good tour of the music facilities, gym, science labs, or whatever your child is interested in, as the guide quite naturally wants to show off the school. (The guide is not likely to be someone who is going to run away or get kicked out next week.) If you can, you can prime your child to ask some questions when it seems appropriate. One thing that you and your child may both want to know is what role the student government has. Your guide should be able to explain that to you. You might ask what the students are most proud of in the school. It is a pleasant question and one that will also tell you what the students value. As you walk around the campus, don't be too fascinated with the dormitory facilities. Be more concerned with what you see students *doing*. As in the section on walking the halls of the public school, pay attention to the number of students you see apparently at work of some kind; talking to teachers; goofing off; plotting mutinies; flirting; hanging around the coke machine; working on their own in a lab after school; engaging in sports; or reading a book in the library.

Admissions Testing

Finally we come to admissions testing, which is, of course, crucial to whether or not your child will be admitted to a particular school. Most boarding schools and some independent day schools at the high school level use the Secondary School Admissions Test, know as the SSAT which your child will take in the eighth or ninth grade before entering private secondary schools. These tests are designed much like the SAT's in that they have reading and mathematics components. How your child does on the SSAT's is, of course, important. It is the percentiles which matter. You might ask the admissions officer what percentiles they look for on the SSAT, to give you some idea of whether your child should be considering this particular school.

In many city private schools, where most admissions take place in kindergarten, schools use the testing service of the Educational Records Bureau (ERB). For entrance to pre-kindergarten or grades 1 and 2, applicants are usually given the individual Stanford-Binet or the Wechsler Test for young children. Above grade 3 they are generally given a written intelligence test. It is common practice for the scores from ERB to be sent to the school, and not reported to the parents themselves. (For more information about this ERB testing program, you can write Educational Records Bureau, 3 East 80 Street, New York, New York 10021.)

Usually parents are advised that it does no good to prepare a child for these tests. We do not quite agree with that statement. We certainly think that if your child has not had much mathematics practice recently, it is a good idea to practice mathematics computation to make sure those skills are polished. We also think that reading is something you can practice, as is vocabulary. We do not think that children should be given the exact same test because a good examiner will notice it and realize that a child has been coached, in which case the test is invalid and you, as a parent, are then under a cloud.

Often the test scores are reported in such broad categories that it is hard for a parent to make much sense of the results. As a parent you're going to be most concerned, or should be, to see that your child aims for a school that is well within your child's range. If your child's IQ is around 105, then you certainly do not want to put that child in a school where the average IQ is 118. Your child is unlikely to succeed, and it would be a cruel thing to do. We urge you to be *very insistent* on getting a good match between your child's ability and the student population's ability. Be frank in discussing this with the admissions officer, because they want to make a good match also. You may ask, if you don't know your child's IQ: "We need to feel that our child is going to be within the average ability level of your school. I understand that your average ability is around 120 in this school. Do John's test scores suggest that he is at this level? Would he be able to move along with the rest of the students?"

This question of match is the *most important* responsibility that parents undertake in choosing a school. It is obviously true that there are exceptions to the rule. There are children who don't do very well on tests who turn out to love the challenge of a highly competitive environment. There are also children who test very high and are very poor scholars. But, in general, it is true that children are miserable, feel like they have failed, and get very depressed in an environment where they cannot succeed, no matter how hard they try. Nothing is more heartrending than seeing perfectly nice youngsters whose learning ability is simply not up to that of the school in which they have been placed. No matter how hard they study, or how hard they work, or how many hours they put in, they simply cannot keep up with the rest of the students. Parents would be very wise to avoid such situations. Should they happen, recognize the signs immediately so that your child can be tested and the match reexamined. On the other hand, a gifted child will need a careful match with a fast-moving school and advanced instructional opportunities.

Picking a school for your child is one of the most important decisions you are going to make. Yet some parents treat it as casually as shopping for an overcoat. Picking the right school means *work*—you are going to have to inform yourself, to do your homework, and to make those school visits during the week, when the school is in session. This means taking time off from your job. It means expense. It means contacting people, talking to strangers, establishing an information network, making phone calls, and learning and recording a lot of information carefully. It means observing carefully, listening carefully in classes, hearing the values that are stated subtly.

Your child, by comparison, is going to spend 3–4 years in an educational environment which you will help him or her to choose. You are choosing another family for your child, a set of foster parents—tutors who will act in your place during some critical years.

Take care, take pains, and take the time to make the best choice you can make.

CHAPTER 13

The Questions Most Frequently Asked About Testing

Do Tests Really Matter?

Yes, they certainly do! They help the school know how much the child has learned. Classroom tests count toward the marks the child will receive. Tests also are used to decide who is admitted where.

How Do I Handle the Child Who Is Tense and Anxious About Tests?

Although some anxiety may be useful to some students for test performance, the stress and competition fostered by today's testing can be a real problem for some students. Placement tests, SAT's, and admission tests present a series of hurdles for many students. Suggestions for handling test anxiety include:

1. Parents should respond in a realistic manner. Do not overreact to test scores.
2. Practicing those skills likey to be tested *does help*. For example, time spent preparing for the SAT with study guides or in special courses helps familiarize students with the format of questions to be asked, the types of vocabulary words that are tested, and the kinds of quantitative problems to be solved. Not only will this practice help students be more at ease in the testing situation, it is also likely to improve their scores.

My Child Is Hampered by Time Limits. What Do I Do?

The child who cannot seem to finish or who answers very few questions may be displaying a sign of slow reading rate, an area you will need to check. If the child is pondering over those questions he or she does not know, he or she should skip over these until other questions have been completed.

Are Tests Culturally Biased?

Toward the culture of the *school,* yes! Most tests children take in school test *school* learning. That is the purpose of these tests.

Should Children Be Given the Results of Tests?

Yes, we feel they should. Children can understand where their performance is strong, where they may need to study more, providing such information allows them to know how they compare realistically to others.

Are Scores Unchanging or Fixed?

Scores *do change.* They can go up and they can go down. They reflect only samples of the pupil's behavior *at the time the test was taken.*

Should a Child Perform at the Same Level in All Subject Areas?

No! Most pupils perform better in some areas than in others, just as most of us are better in some skills, and poorer in others.

What Is the Difference Between Assessment and Testing?

Assessment refers to a broad range of procedures used in schools to help understand children, including interviews, questionnaires, observations, ratings, and inventories, as well as tests. Tests are only one part of the assessment procedure.

What is the Purpose of Statewide and Systemwide Achievement Testing?

Statewide and systemwide achievement testing programs are used for several purposes:

1. To monitor achievement levels of schools in learning areas such as reading, mathematics, and writing.

2. To provide information to teachers as to progress of their pupils in these areas as compared to other pupils of the same age and grade.
3. To assess whether or not minimal competency levels have been met that qualify pupils to graduate. In some states, pupils have to meet a minimum level of competency in basic skills before they can receive their diplomas.

What Is an "Overachiever"?

This term is often used with children who perform (achieve) better on a day-to-day basis in the classroom than tests of ability would suggest. Often these children are highly motivated and spend a lot of time studying and working, both at home and at school. However, the term really is inaccurate. Whatever level a pupil achieves *is* what he or she can do. One cannot *over*achieve. One can achieve higher than some people expect, or certain tests predict, but that only proves that these expectations and predictions were wrong.

What Is an "Underachiever"?

This term refers to the child who is performing below what tests of ability would predict. Many such children are now referred to as *learning disabled* if they are performing 1½–2 years below grade level, yet show normal levels of ability on tests of intelligence.

What Is Mastery Testing?

Mastery testing tests the precise content and skills which a child has mastered, in which the child has received instruction. This means that mastery testing must be carefully linked to exactly what has been taught. The teacher uses these carefully sequenced tests to measure the pupil's mastery of skills. The focus of this kind of test is not on a child's score, but on those skills the pupil has acquired or in which the pupil encounters difficulty. The results lead to planning the next skill that the pupil will learn. These tests can be retaken as often as necessary until the pupil achieves the mastery level specified, such as 80, or 85, or 90 percent mastery level, meaning 80, or 85, or 90 percent correct performance.

What Is the Future of Tests?

Most educators, most students, and most parents, would get rid of all examinations and all tests, if this step would not create more problems than keeping the tests themselves. Almost no one likes to take a test, most teachers dislike giving and correcting them, and most parents worry about tests for their children.

Tests were invented because they served a purpose. Most people do not recall how decisions were made in schools *before* tests were developed. If a teacher thought a child slow, the teacher might have kept that child back, or even caused the child to be dropped from school. Tests were invented to reduce arbitrary or prejudicial judgments, and to increase the objectivity with which decisions about students were made. So tests filled a need.

As the demand rose for more and more students to obtain more and more education, and as the competition for admission increased, tests became the object of attack for the anger students felt about the selection process that determined if or where they went to college or graduate school.

As population pressures decrease in the school age group, as competition drops and college classrooms remain unfilled, and as many small private colleges go bankrupt, we can expect to hear less resentment about test scores.

Tests are far from perfect, but they are still a fairer way to select pupils than on teacher judgment. On a test, each pupil has the same chance to perform. With human judgment, there is always the personal reaction, pro or con.

How Seriously Should Parents Take Test Scores?

In our opinion, *seriously*. Why? Because test scores, especially when there are several of them over time, are the most objective evidence parents can get about the school ability of their child. Teachers may like your child or not; they may estimate your child's ability correctly, or not. Parents need some objective measure to tell what is reasonable to expect in school achievement for their child. One child may be at the 25th percentile in school IQ tests, and achieve around the 25th percentile in achievement tests, which represents as maximum a performance—for that child—as one who is at the 80th percentile in school IQ tests, and achieves around the 80th percentile on achievement tests. Each child is doing the best they can in terms of their natural school ability.

Parents have a right to know their children's test results, to understand them, to use these results wisely in setting expectations, and in educational planning.

What's the Truth About the SAT's and Discrimination?

Now for a word regarding the SAT test scores, about which there has been a great deal of controversy. SAT means Scholastic Aptitude Test.

Let us start with the fact that most colleges want some measure of a student's ability to succeed scholastically in college, beyond his or her high school academic record. Why aren't school grades enough to judge admission to a college? Because school grades are not the same from school to school, or even class to class. In school A, there may be a high rate of grade inflation, so that as much as 50 percent of the students get A's. In school B, which prides itself on being a tough grading school, A's may be a rarity. Two students, one from school A and one from school B, may have the same level of scholastic ability and be equally able to succeed in college, but the student from school A will have a clear grade advantage over the student from school B.

To try to compensate for differences among schools in grading policy and in degree of difficulty, objective tests were introduced on a large scale before World War II to help college admissions officers choose students more fairly. In the example above, if the two students from school A and B had scored roughly the same in a college aptitude test, then the admissions officer might have accepted both, even though their school grades reflected different school academic policies.

This attempt to provide a uniform and objective measure of college aptitude was the impetus for the development of the college board testing program. High school students take an aptitude test (SAT—Scholastic Aptitude Test) and a Preliminary Scholastic Aptitude Test (PSAT) or The American College Testing Program (ACT). They also can take College Boards in specific subjects, such as in English, the sciences, mathematics, and languages. If a student does exceptionally well in one of these specific subjects, the student can apply for advanced standing in that subject in the college he or she attends, and be allowed to skip over the lower level course.

The purpose behind the development of the SAT's and the College Boards was to add objectivity and reliability to the college selection process. What has happened since then is that these tests have been viewed as the obstacles to college admission by many students, especially those who have argued that the tests discriminate against minority students. In one sense, *all* measures of performance, from the simplest letter grade to the most artfully built test, *discriminate* in the sense that they are *intended* to discriminate among the performances of students, some receiving A, some B, some C, some D, and some F.

One charge that has been made against the SAT's is that coaching does increase scores, whereas the Educational Testing Service, the company that produces the test, has argued in the past that coaching does not help. The evidence at this writing suggests that certain kinds of coaching do indeed raise scores. The most effective coaching appears to be exactly what one would predict—long-term coaching rather than short-term, lasting several weeks or months. With coaching of this type, assuming it to consist of high-quality instruction, scores on the SAT's have gone up 50 points or better. Educational Testing Service now advises[1] that 8 hours of coaching will provide an average increase on the mean score of 10 points; after 19 hours, 20 points; and after 45 hours, 30 points. Students usually gain 10–20 points on their own when taking the test a second time.

Another argument against the SAT's is that a student has no access to information about his performance, other than a score. Machine scoring can include errors. One result of this criticism has been to open up information about test performance to students in statewide legislations. The argument for "truth in testing" as the bill has been called, which allows students to see the test items and answers against their own performance, is a strong one, namely that people in our society should have the right to know how they are being judged, especially in anything as important as admission to college. Under the provisions of current legislation, students in some states may receive their answers as well as those the test makers deemed correct, so that they may review their scores and how they were computed. Test makers object to this opening up of test items because it will require them to develop new test items each year.

A third charge against the SAT's and other tests that are used to make admissions judgments are that such tests discriminate against minority students. It is true that minority students, on the *whole*, score less well on these tests than the white majority students. Some argue that this is because the tests involve items of information less likely to be known by minority applicants, and therefore that such items are discriminatory. The counterargument is that the test items are chosen because of their ability to predict academic success in college or graduate school, which is what the tests are supposed to do. Even though an item may seem farfetched, if it helps to predict school success, then it is a useful item to the test developer. The test developer wants to build a test from items that will predict future school performance, because that is the purpose of the test. The student who comes from a minority background may find such items hard or unfamiliar, and feel the items are discriminatory.

It seems to us that this discrimination argument about what predicts performance is often unrealistic. If we want to know if Jane or Manuel are good at running, then we would ask them to run. We would not ask them questions about the physiology of running. If we want to know if Margarita or Ping would be good at gardening, we would probably give them a trial at gardening with instruction, to see how quickly they learned. If we want to know if children will learn to read quickly or slowly, the best prediction would be a trial of reading instruction to see how quickly or slowly they learned. Schools like to group youngsters for instruction in many subjects, so schools may use a reading readiness test which will predict, reasonably well, who will be the quick reading learner and who will be slow. Pupils then may be grouped for instruction according to their speed of learning.

[1]*New York Times*, December 23, 1980.

If we want to predict *school* performance at any level, from elementary to graduate level, we will be more accurate at prediction if we test those skills that are required for *school* success. To be successful in a public school today, as it was yesterday, a student is required to read well and quickly, and to comprehend what he or she has read; to handle numbers easily and accurately; to listen with comprehension to what is said; to follow written directions correctly; to write quickly and comprehensibly; to understand abstract reasoning; to use symbols correctly; to utilize reference sources quickly and accurately; and to take examinations successfully. These are some of the skills tapped by these school aptitude tests.

The argument really is about *what is needed for school success,* not about the tests that purport to predict success. As long as schools are organized as they are, teach substantially the same curricula, and use the same criteria for successful academic performance, then school success itself is going to consist of skills that some will argue are discriminatory. (These are the same skills tested by the tests.) As long as school success depends upon such skills as reading, writing, arithmetic, abstract reasoning, listening, and following directions—as long as that is true—then school success will be achieved by students with these skills, and those with different skills will be less successful. This is not to say that school skills are better or worse than the skills required for inner city survival, for making pottery, for painting a mural, for growing vegetables, or for raising sheep. Each has its own set of skills.

What most people in our society have believed is that the skills required for school success are also the skills needed for life after school in jobs, in leisure activities, in hobbies, in cultural appreciation, in citizenship participation, and in self-development. The formal school skills of reading, writing, numbering, reasoning, and so on are skills that are needed to learn most new written information, whether it is information for employment or for one's own development. This view has been challenged by the widespread use of television to inform the public, as well as to entertain it. It is true that many job-related and self-development skills can now be taught by visual and auditory methods through television and newer electronic media, and taught effectively, as compared with the traditional written form. As this trend increases, school skills will change, or be challenged as less relevant.

Why Have SAT Scores Gone Down?

A popular subject in the media has been the report of the recent decline in SAT scores, often with the implication that this is an indictment of our schools, of society, of children, or of parents.

First, the facts: Have SAT scores declined? Yes, they have. When the test was first developed, the range of scores for the SAT and all College Board tests was 200–800, derived from the distribution of college applicants in 1941. The average score of 500 was set as the performance that would have been earned by the average 1941 applicant. (This was applied to current SAT scores through special statistical techniques.[2]) Up through the late 1960s, the average score was above 500. Beginning in 1969, the average SAT has declined to scores around 450 for both verbal and mathematics.[3]

Many reasons have been given for this decline, some of them substantial, some not. One reason offered has been that a wider range of lower ability students is now taking the SAT's, whereas before a more restricted group took them. This argument has been refuted by a study which showed that scores have declined for students across the board, so that it is a widespread effect, not one restricted to one segment of the student population. There have been speculations that lowered SAT scores reflect the turbulence and change in standards within our society as a whole, since the drop has paralleled the Vietnam War, Watergate, and the movement of many students against traditional academic standards. Another factor may be the rise of television watching. Students average almost 30 hours a week of television watching. It is clear that most students cannot watch television and simultaneously study or read effectively. So one has to speculate what that 30 hours of time taken away may mean to school achievement. It is also quite possible that parents and teachers are both less demanding about homework than before the 1960s. Whatever the causes may be, they are probably part of the fabric of our whole society, not a special effect created by schools alone—just as the decline in industrial productivity during the same period can possibly be attributed to similar causes. Drops in SAT scores, over ten years, by all levels of ability, suggests so broad a change that the causes must be complex and broad themselves.

[2]Cronbach, *op. cit*, p. 97.

[3]*New York Times*, September 9, 1979.

Appendices

A: A Calendar for School Testing   168

B: Interpreting Grade Equivalent Scores   170

C: Percentiles and Their Numerical Meaning   172

D: Percentiles and Their Qualitative Meaning   173

E: Converting Stanines to Percentiles   174

F: If You Want More Information: Suggested Readings   175

G: Admissions Standards to Colleges   177

    Table 1: A Survey of Policies and Practices   177

    Table 2: Minimum Academic Standards of Admission   178

    Table 3: Characteristics and Credentials Considered Very
           Important Factors in Admissions Decisions   178

A Calendar of School Testing

Grade	Type of Testing	What it Measures	When to Expect Testing
Preschool	(1) Screening to plan teaching	Identification of child's strengths and weakness across learning areas	Anytime, but usually at beginning of school year
	(2) Screening to identify potential problems	Identification of areas needing more comprehensive testing	Anytime
	(3) Diagnostic testing	Comprehensive testing in areas of concern: vision, hearing, motor, language skills, self-help skills, ability to deal with group situations, and the like	Anytime
Kinder-garten	(1) Screening to plan teaching	As in preschool	Beginning of school year
	(2) Screening to identify potential problems	As in preschool	Anytime
	(3) Diagnostic testing	As in preschool	Anytime
	(4) Readiness testing	Testing to determine whether child has mastered skills necessary for success in beginning reading and mathematics	End of school year
	(5) Evaluation of progress	Testing to evaluate progress related to (1)–(3)	End of school year
Grade 1	(1)–(3) As in previous years		
	(4) Readiness testing	Testing to determine whether child has mastered prerequisite skills for success in beginning reading and mathematics	Beginning of school year
	(5) Mastery testing	Testing to determine mastery of learning objectives	Ongoing
	(6) Achievement	Progress tested in the reading and mathematics achievement areas	End of school year

Grade	Type of Testing	What it Measures	When to Expect Testing
Grades 2–5	(1)–(3) As in previous years		
	(4) Mastery testing	Testing to determine mastery of learning objectives	Ongoing
	(5) Achievement testing	To monitor progress in subjects	Fall (October–November) or Mid-year (January–February) or End of year (April–May)
	(6) Ability (IQ) testing	To determine learning rate	Every 2–3 years
	(7) Diagnostic achievement testing	In-depth test of progress, strengths and weakness in individual subject areas	May be a regular part of the school program in the fall, or with children encountering difficulty with a school subject, as needed
Grades 6–8	(1) Mastery testing	Testing to determine mastery of learning objectives	Ongoing
	(2) Diagnostic testing	Comprehensive testing in areas of concern	As needed
	(3) Achievement testing	To monitor progress in subjects	Fall or mid-year or end of year
	(4) Ability testing	To determine learning rate	Every 2–3 years
	(5) Tests of interest	To determine interests of pupils relative to vocational planning	One time during grade 7 or 8
	(6) Tests of aptitude	To determine learning abilities for program and placement planning	One time during grade 7 or 8
Grades 9–10	(1)–(4) As in grades 6–8		
	(5) Tests of interest		Possibly given one time during this period
	(6) Test of aptitude		Possibly given one time during this period
Grades 11–12	(1)–(4) As in grades 6–8		
	(5) Test of interests		Possibly given one time during this period
	(6) PSAT: Preliminary Scholastic Aptitude Test	Preliminary estimate of aptitude for college level work	Late fall or early spring of junior year
	(7) Tests of special aptitude	Testing for ability in vocational areas or of special abilities for program planning	Generally late fall or early spring
	(8) SAT: Scholastic Aptitude Test ACT: American College Testing Program SCAT: School and College Ability Tests	Assessment of aptitude for college level academic work	Fall of senior year

Interpreting Grade Equivalent Scores (GES)

Step 1. Determine the number of months of the school year that have passed. They are expressed as decimals, .1 to .9. Add to grade your child is in.

.1	.2	.3	.4	.5	.6	.7	.8	.9
Sept. 15 to Oct. 14	Oct. 15 to Nov. 14	Nov. 15 to Dec. 14	Dec. 15 to Jan. 14	Jan. 15 to Feb. 14	Feb. 15 to Mar. 14	Mar. 15 to Apr. 14	Apr. 15 to May 14	May 14 to June 14

Step 2. Record the grade equivalent score and percentile for each area on the standardized test.

			Grade Equivalent Scores Received on Each Area of Standardized Test		
	Pupil's Grade	Number of Months Passed of School Year	Subtest	Grade Equivalent Score (GES) GES	Percentile
(ex.) Your Child	4	3	Reading	5.4	88
	___	___	___	___	___
	___	___	___	___	___
		___	___	___	___
		___	___	___	___

Step 3. Write below each GES and percentile in appropriate column. This will give you a quick chart to show strengths and weaknesses.

	Subtest Name	−2 Years Needing Attention	−1 Year Below Average	Current Grade and Months Average	+1 Year Above Average	+2 Years Superior
(ex).	Reading				5.4 (88)	

Note: The meaning of GES changes as the pupil spends more time in school. To be behind 1 grade level in reading when the child is in grade 2 is to be much further behind than when the child is in grade 8.

Percentiles and Their Numerical Meaning

90th percentile ——— → 90% scored below your child and 10% above.

80th percentile ——— → 80% scored below your child and 20% above.

70th percentile ——— → 70% scored below your child and 30% above.

60th percentile ——— → 60% scored below your child and 40% above.

50th percentile ——— → 50% Your child scored at the mean of all children taking this test; 50% of the group scored below your child and 50% above

40th percentile ——— → 40% scored below your child and 60% above.

30th percentile ——— → 30% scored below your child and 70% above.

20th percentile ——— → 20% scored below your child and 80% above.

10th percentile ——— → 10% scored below your child and 90% above.

Percentiles and Their Qualitative Meaning*

Subject Area

						Very	Excel-
		Some-	Average	Good	Good	lent
Great		what	Under-	Under-	Under-	Under-
Difficulty	Difficulty	Below	standing	standing	standing	standing

Percentile*

	.01	10	20	30	40	50	60	70	80	90	99.9
	|	|	|	|	|	|	|	|	|	|	|
	|	|	|	|	|	|	|	|	|	|	|
	|	|	|	|	|	|	|	|	|	|	|
	|	|	|	|	|	|	|	|	|	|	|
	|	|	|	|	|	|	|	|	|	|	|
	|	|	|	|	|	|	|	|	|	|	|
	|	|	|	|	|	|	|	|	|	|	|
	|	|	|	|	|	|	|	|	|	|	|

*Each percentile on the chart tells you how your child's score compares with other children taking the test who were part of the standardization group.

Read—"On _____ test, my child scored above _____ *percent* of children taking this test."

Converting Stanines to Percentiles

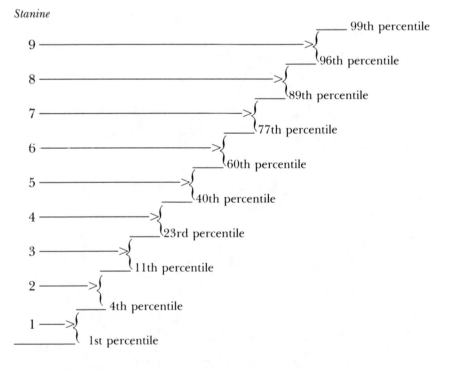

Stanine

9 — 99th percentile

96th percentile

8 — 89th percentile

7 — 77th percentile

6 — 60th percentile

5 — 40th percentile

4 — 23rd percentile

3 — 11th percentile

2 — 4th percentile

1 — 1st percentile

Read: "My child, scoring at the _____ stanine, scored between the _____ and _____ percentile. For example, a child with a stanine of 5 has a score the falls between the 40th and 60th percentile.

If You Want More Information: Suggested Readings

Study Skills

CARMEN, R.A., AND ADAMS, W.R. *Study Skills: A Student's Guide for Survival.* New York: John Wiley, 1972.

Particularly useful in identifying different types of clue words in reading material such as those that signal change of ideas, emphasis, summary, and conclusion.

SPARGO, E. *The Now Student.* Providence, RI: Jamestown Publishers, 1977.

Describes the "reading process and study skills." Includes topics such as note-taking and memory techniques. Also directs student to time and chart reading speeds. Intended for grades 11 and 12, but many students in grades 9 and 10 will find this helpful.

WALSH, F. *The Regis Study Skills Guide.* New York: Regis/High School, 1977 (55 E. 84th St., New York, N.Y. 10028).

Describes useful procedures for such areas as concentration, organization of time, reading speed and comprehension and developing new vocabulary, memory, note-taking, and test-taking. Intended for the high school level.

WRIGHTSTONE, J.W. *How to Be a Better Student.* Chicago: Science Research Associates, 1972 (1956).

Checklist of 39 skills which range from note-taking to using the library. Study tips are presented in such areas as improving memory, comprehension, reading maps, graphs and tables, and preparing for tests. Intended for junior high and high school levels.

ZIFFERBLATT, S.M. *Improving Study and Homework Behaviors.* Champaign, Ill.: Research Press, 1970 (2612 N. Mattis Ave., Champaign, Ill. 61820).

Focus on helping parents improve their children's study and homework behaviors. Basic focus is on managing behavior through reinforcement principles.

Educational and Psychological Measurement

The titles that follow present detailed accounts of evaluation procedures used in education and psychology—along with their strengths and limitations. Issues of test reliability and validity are addressed throughout these books:

ANASTASI, A. *Psychological Testing*. 5th ed. New York: MacMillan, 1981.

CRONBACH, L.J. *Essentials of Psychological Testing*, 3rd ed. New York: Harper & Row. 1970.

McLOUGHLIN, J.A., AND LEWIS, R.B. *Assessing Special Students: Strategies and Procedures*. Columbus, Ohio; Charles E. Merrill Publishing Company, 1981.

MEHRENS, W.A., AND LEHMANN, D.J. *Measurement and Evaluation in Education and Psychology*. New York: Holt, Rinehart and Winston, 1973.

MERCER, C.D. *Children and Adolescents with Learning Disabilities*. Columbus, Ohio: Charles E. Merrill, 1979.

SALVIA, J., AND YSSELDYKE, J.E. *Assessment in Special and Remedial Education*, 2nd ed. Boston: Houghton–Mifflin, 1981.

WALLACE, G., AND LARSEN, S.C. *Educational Assessment of Learning Problems: Testing for Teaching*. Boston: Allyn & Bacon, 1973.

Materials Directed to Parent Audiences

DYER, H.S. *Parents can Understand Testing*. Columbia, Md.: National Committee for Citizens in Education, 1980 (Suite 410, Wildlake Village Green, Columbia, Md. 21044. $3.50).

Presents an overview of tests given in school and raises issues pertinent to testing in educational settings. Of particular value is a section that lists minimum competency tests, their purpose, and levels used in various states.

Parents' Guide to Understanding Tests. Monterey, California: CTB/McGraw-Hill, 1976.

Test Service Notebook 34, *Some Things Parents Should Know About Testing*. New York: Psychological Corporation, 1959. (Marketing Division, 757 Third Ave., New York, NY 10017. no charge).

Admissions Standards to Colleges

Table 1
A Survey of Policies and Practices at 1,463 Institutions—General Admissions Practices

	All Institu-tions (%)	2-year Public (%)	2-year Private (%)	4-year Public (%)	4-year Private (%)
Open door[1]	34	89	35	20	8
Selective[2]	56	9	60	70	77
Competitive[3]	8	1	5	10	13
Not reported	2	1	0	0	2

[1]Admit all who wish to attend without review of conventional academic qualifications.

[2]Admit a majority of applicants who meet some specified level of academic achievement or other qualification beyond high school graduation.

[3]Admit only a limited number of those applicants who meet specified level of academic achievement or other qualifications beyond high school graduation.

Source: *The Chronicle of Higher Education,* January 19, 1981, p. 8. Reprinted by permission.

Table 2
Minimum Academic Standards of Admission

	All Institu- tions	2-year Public	2-year Private	4-year Public	4-year Private
High school grade average	40%[1]	6%	46%	43%	58%
Average requirement	2.0	1.9	1.9	2.0	2.0
High school class rank	29%	2%	23%	33%	44%
Average percentile requirement	43	39	42	40	44
Scholastic Aptitude Test score	30%	4%	22%	39%	42%
Average SAT score requirement[2] (verbal plus mathematical)	740	650	617	740	754
American College Testing score	24%	2%	21%	30%	36%
Average ACT composite score requirement	16.2	15.5	14.8	16.2	16.4

[1]Percentages refer to percentage of institutions reporting a particular practice.
[2]Note the minimum SAT scores mean verbal *plus* mathematical score, for a total of the two scores. Thus 740, set as the minimum for all 4-year public undergraduate institutions, means such scores as verbal 370 plus mathematics 370 — total of 740, or any other combination adding to 740.
Source: *The Chronicle of Higher Education,* January 19, 1981, p. 8. Reprinted by permission.

Table 3
Characteristics and Credentials Considered Very Important Factors in Admissions Decisions

	All Institu- tions (%)[1]	2-year Public (%)	2-year Private (%)	4-year Public (%)	4-year Private (%)
Academic performance in high school	65	21	77	77	84
Aptitude test scores	44	10	38	63	55
Achievement test scores	5	2	5	4	7
Recommendation					
High school	13	1	22	4	7
Church					
Employer or others	7	1	15	1	13
Interview with faculty member, alumnus, staff member, student, or other	15	5	27	6	23
Personal essay or statement	7	1	4	3	13
Health statement	6	4	14	5	7
Applicant's place of residence	4	8	0	6	1
Documentation of previous work	5	2	4	6	7
Pattern of high school subjects	26	8	21	25	38
Declaration of major	9	10	11	9	7
Ability to pay tuition and fees	4	4	9	1	4

[1]Percentages refer to the percentage of institutions reporting each factor; e.g., 84% of the 4-year private undergraduate institutions consider academic performance in high school a very important factor in admissions decisions.
Source: *The Chronicle of Higher Education,* January 19, 1981, p. 8. Reprinted by permission.

Glossary of Testing Terms

ability   Talent; power to do something.

achievement test   Measure of what pupil has learned to do, based on past instruction in school subjects such as reading, mathematics, and science.

age norms   Norm that tells the average *age* of children getting the same number of items right on a test, which is called the *educational age* or age equivalent score.

age score   The age equivalent for a particular score on a standardized test.

aptitude   Measure of natural ability or talent for a given school area.

assessment   A variety of procedures for understanding the pupil, including interviews, questionnaires, rating forms, observation, inventories, and tests.

assessor   The person administering a test; examiner.

at risk   A term used to describe a child who on the basis of several tests is thought likely to encounter difficulty in later school learning.

average   See mean.

basal   First age level on a test at which all tasks are performed correctly, thus forming the base of a child's performance, thus "basal."

band of scores   Scores presented as falling in a range of scores rather than at one point, which helps avoid the problem of unwarranted comparison between close scores.

battery of tests   Group of several separate tests given to the child at the same time so as to be able to compare the child's functioning in several areas.

behavioral objective   Learning goal stated in terms of the *exact* behaviors pupils need to demonstrate in order to achieve (pass) that goal.

Buckley amendment   Congressional legislation giving parents the right to see their children's school records.

CA   See chronological age.

ceiling   The highest level which the student passed on a test.

child find   Procedures used to locate preschool children who might need assistance to prevent later problems in school learning.

classroom test   Test made up by the child's classroom teacher; also called teacher tests or teacher-made tests.

chronological age or CA   Child's age in years and months.

cognitive   Tests which assess the child's development of thinking skills and concepts such as comprehension of word meanings, ability to follow directions, and to see relationships.

CR   See criterion-referenced.

criterion-referenced or CR   Testing that relates the child's progress to an educational criterion, usually the mastery of behavioral objectives.

cumulative record   The school record maintained over the years as the child progresses through school, to which information is added cumulatively. Generally contains grades, attendance record, test scores, and sometimes the health record.

completion questions   See fill in the blank.

DAT   The Differential Aptitude Test is a test of several abilities given early in high school for educational planning.

developmental assessment   Observation of children's development over time as they participate in different activities.

developmental scales   The child's performance on a series of different tasks is observed and compared to the development of other children the same age. The tasks are ordered from less difficult to more difficult. The ability to perform them depends on the increasing physical and mental development of the child.

diagnostic testing   Comprehensive testing of the child, usually done by a trained specialist, to find out if a school problem exists and its source.

EA   See educational age.

educational age or EA   Scores expressed in terms of the average chronological age of the child obtaining each score on a test.

educational prescriptions   Specific learning activities recommended to help the child.

educational quotient   The relationship of the child's educational age to his or her chronological age.

essay test   A test that requires the child to respond by writing a detailed explanation or comparison. The organization of ideas and the scope and completeness of the answer is important, as well as neatness and handwriting.

evaluation   Testing that weighs how effectively an instructional program is teaching.

expressive language   Pupil's ability to use words and sentences which include nouns, verbs, adjectives, and prepositions to express their thoughts.

fill in the blank questions   This type of question requires the child to fill in the missing information. "America was discovered in____." is one example of fill in the blank questions.

floor   The lowest level which the pupil passed on a test. This is the same as the "basal."

FSIQ   See full scale IQ.

Full scale IQ or FSIQ   An IQ score based on both portions (verbal and performance) of the Wechsler Intelligence Scales.

GCI   General cognitive index, a form of IQ score.

Grade equivalent scores or GES or GS   A pupil's score on a test is converted into grades and months of the school year. The child's score is compared to the typical child at that grade and month receiving each score on the test. Grade equivalent scores should be converted to percentile ranks so that scores from one test can be compared to another.

GE, GES   See grade equivalent scores.

grade norms   The average score on a standardized test obtained by an average child with each increasing month in school.

group test   Test administered to children as a group, usually in the classroom.

individual test   Test designed to be administered to a child in a one-to-one relationship between the child and the trained examiner.

instructional objective   See behavioral objectives.

intelligence   Overall ability to reason, think, and solve problems.

intelligence or IQ tests   Tests of a child's brightness or quickness to learn school material. These tests include tasks which sample behaviors (verbal, nonverbal, and numerical) related to general school ability. They are one type of aptitude test that helps to predict the child's ability to learn school work.

IQ   Intelligence quotient. A score from a test measuring a child's intelligence. The average IQ score is 100.

interest tests   Tests of a pupil's interests, such as mechanical, artistic, outdoor, and so on.

inventory   An inventory is a questionnaire which typically includes many items on one subject such as a child's interests or attitudes.

IS   Independent (or private) school.

item   A question on a test.

LA   Learning age; see educational age.

language tests   Tests that help determine a pupil's skill in understanding and using language.

learning age or LA   See educational age.

loc.   Local. Abbreviation used on test result reports.

local norms   Interpretation of test scores based on how other pupils in the same community perform in order to develop local (community) levels of expectation.

LQ   A learning quotient, a form of IQ.

MA   See mental age.

machine scored test   The child writes on the test booklet or on an answer sheet using a special pencil. The answer sheets are then sent away and scored by machine.

mastery tests   Tests measuring the child's mastery of behavioral objectives for a curricular unit, usually organized by level of difficulty.

matching test question   Child matches material presented on one list to material presented on another.

mental age or MA   The number of items answered correctly on a test of ability, divided by the child's chronological age. A mental age of 100 corresponds to the average performance of a child of any chronological age.

mean, M or $\overline{X}$ Arithmetic average of all scores on a test. The scores of all children taking the test are added up and then divided by the number of children.

motor test   Test that assesses a pupil's ability to move and coordinate his/her body and manipulate objects.

m reas   mechanical reasoning. Abbreviation used on test result reports. Test of ability to visualize mechanical operations of pulleys, weights, gears, leverage, and so on.

multiple choice test   Child selects *one* answer from among several answers on a test such as, "We celebrate Independence Day on *a)* Feb. 22, *b)* May 31, *c)* July 4, *d)* Oct. 12."

N (abil) or NA   Numerical ability.

nat'l.   National. Abbreviation commonly used.

nonverbal   Items on tests that do not require an answer in words, such as similarities or differences in designs.

no rt   Number right, or answered correctly. Abbreviation commonly used.

no pos   Total number of items possible to answer on a test. Abbreviation commonly used.

normal curve   A way to show the normal distribution graphically of scores of people taking a test. Sometimes called the bell-shaped curve because it is shaped like a bell.

normal distribution   See normal curve.

norm   Translations of scores into some comparative measure (grade equivalent scores, percentile ranks, stanines, or standard scores) that allow the individual's test score to be compared to that of a comparable group. Norms can be developed for the nation as a whole, the local community, for private schools, for children with special needs, and so on.

normal level   Average level.

normative group   A representative group of children on whose performance the test has been developed and standardized. The scores of this group of children serve as the yardstick against which to compare the scores of others.

norm-referenced tests or NR   Tests that permit the comparison of an individual child's test score with the average score of a representative group of children of the same age or grade.

NR   See norm-referenced; abbreviation also used for numerical reasoning.

NR   Numerical reasoning; (also norm-referenced). Test of ability to reason with quantitative symbols.

objective test   A test on which the answers, usually to short questions such as multiple choice and true-false, are scored either right or wrong.

observational assessment   Assessment of children's behavior and skills through observation carried out in the natural setting of the classroom or playground. Observation can be carried out on an informal basis or on a structured basis, such as using a checklist of what to observe.

percentile band   Range of scores in which the child's "true" score is likely to fall, given the error known to exist in any test.

percentile rank or PR   PR is a score that tells how a child ranks on a test in relationship to others in the group taking the test. It tells the percent of children receiving a score at or below the one reported for the child. A percentile rank of 68 means that the child scored at a level at or above 68 percent of children taking that test. Likewise a percentile rank of 20 means that the child scored at a level or above 20 percent of children.

percent score   The percent of questions answered correctly on a test.

perceptual-motor   Also called visual-motor; see visual-motor.

performance IQ or PIQ   IQ score based on questions which do not require a verbal response, such as putting pieces of a puzzle together.

permanent record   See *cumulative record*. This record is both permanent and cumulative.

personality test   Tests which assess personality. Personality tests include adjustment and behavior inventories and rating scales.

PIQ   Performance IQ (as compared to verbal IQ).

potential   Capacity to learn, latent ability; often misused as tests cannot test potential, only what has been acquired.

power test   Test which most children have enough time to finish, and which, therefore, measures how much they have learned rather than how fast they can answer under timed circumstances.

PR   Percentile rank.

PRI   Primary.

profile   Graphic picture of scores from a test which aids in comparing relative strengths and weaknesses.

prognostic test   A test that helps predict performance in the future in a given skill.

projective test   Tests in which the person responds to nonstructured material, such as inkblots, or draws, or tells stories about ambiguous pictures. Projective tests assume that a person's projections are indicative of that person's personality.

PS   Public school.

quantitative   The understanding of mathematical concepts and computation.

quartile   One quarter of the scores on a test such as the lowest 25 percent of scores = the lowest quartile and the top 25 percent of scores = the top quartile.

questionnaires   Like inventories, a series of written questions to which the student replies in writing. The questionnaire may ask about attitudes, prior events, facts, and so on.

range   Range is the distance between the lowest and the highest score actually received on a given test.

rate   Speed with which one completes a task, such as rate of learning new material, or rate of reading story passages.

rating forms (scales)   A questionnaire in which one rates a quality by a numerical scale or series of adjectives.

raw score   The number of actual items correct on a test.

readiness tests   Test for the matured ability to benefit from instruction such as kindergarten readiness or reading readiness. These tests attempt to measure whether or not children have developed the skills thought to be necessary for success at a given level.

receptive language   Pupils' ability to understand words and sentences that are spoken by others.

reliability   Consistency with which a test measures a child's understanding or behavior with the same score on two or more occasions. The higher the consistency, the higher the reliability.

remedial   Special instructional procedures aimed at remedying, or correcting, a learning problem.

representative sample   A sample of students to whom the test is given initially which represents the type of student for whom the test is intended. Usually a representative sample includes factors such as age, sex, race, socioeconomic background, and geographic region of the country.

SA   Social age.

SAT   Scholastic Aptitude Test.

screening   Identification of the skills of pupils at an initial stage so as to separate those who have such skills for instruction from those who do not, who then receive special instruction. Screening is also used as the initial procedure to identify those children who need diagnostic testing.

SD   Standard deviation; a measure of variability among scores.

self-help   Ability to take care of self and manage without help, such as putting on clothing unassisted.

SEM   See standard error of measurement.

SES   Socioeconomic status.

short answer test   Test questions requiring a short answer, generally only one or a few sentences.

social   Social skills of a young age, self-help skills such as tying one's shoes and the child's ability to interact with others such as "can play in a group"; with older pupils, social interaction skills such as "responsibility," "cooperation and leadership ability," would be viewed.

social age or SA   The age equivalent of the typical child receiving each score on a test measuring social skills.

speech   Child's ability to produce sounds and words correctly.

speed test   See timed test.

Sp Rel   Spatial relations. Abbreviation used on test result reports.

Sta   Stanine. See definition of stanine.

standard   Something established as a basis for comparison, such as the passing score on a statewide test for graduation from high school.

standard deviation or SD   A measure of how much scores on a test vary around the average.

standard error of measurement or SEM   The degree to which a person's score would vary if the same test were taken over and over again.

standard score   A type of score which is based on the mean and standard deviation that allows comparison of a child's performance from one test to another.

standardized tests   Tests given under uniform conditions, using the same directions, materials, and time limits, to groups of typical children across the country.

stanine   One form of reporting test scores by dividing all the test scores into 9 parts. Stanines range from a low of 1 to a high of 9 with the average being 5.

subtests   Smaller parts of a larger test.

survey test   A test that provides an overall measure of an area.

teacher-made test   See *classroom test.*

timed test   A test which is timed, therefore in which speed of answering is important.

TOT   Total. Abbreviation commonly used.

true-false test   Test made up of questions to which the child has to respond by indicating whether they are true or false.

truth-in-testing   Legislation giving students the right to obtain a copy of the questions and their answers on those tests required for admission to higher education.

V   Verbal.

validity   The extent to which a test measures what it is supposed to measure.

variation in scores   A person's performance (score) on a test varies from one testing time to another due to differences in responding, attention, well-being, motivation, and so on.

verbal IQ or VIQ   IQ score based on questions that require a spoken or written answer, therefore, "verbal" IQ.

Voc   Vocabulary. Abbreviation commonly used.

VIQ   See verbal IQ.

V-M   See visual motor.

visual motor   Test items that are thought to tap a child's ability to coordinate vision and physical movement, especially the fine movements requiring hand-eye coordination.

vocational testing   Testing to determine a pupil's aptitudes, preferences, and interests which can aid in making a vocational decision.